He Came Incognito

How Jesus Christ is Relevant
to Your Life Today—and Always!

by

Rev. Oscar Smith

He Came Incognito

by Oscar Smith

© MMXIII Oscar Smith, *all rights reserved worldwide*

No part of this publication may be reproduced or transmitted in any form or by any means, mechanical or electronic, including photocopying and recording, or by any information storage and retrieval system, without permission in writing from author or publisher.

ISBN: 978-1466365452 Paperback

Published by:
Parthenon Marketing Inc
2400 Crestmoor Rd #36
Nashville TN 37215 USA

info@ehaste.com
+1-615-662-3169
fax: +1-615-369-9479

 For more on Rev. Oscar Smith or to invite him to speak visit www.Just1King.com

A portion of all proceeds is put to His work in the ministries of Gratitude Life and www.AdotcomChurch.com.

LEGAL NOTICES: All rights reserved. This book is protected by the copyright laws of the Unted States of America. Unless otherwise identified, Scripture quotations are from the Holy Bible, New King James Version, New American Standard and New International Version. Respectfully, editorial committee has chosen against the standard publishing style which does not capitalize certain pronouns in Scripture that refer to the Father, Son, and Holy Spirit. Certain terms related to Satan are not capitalized; as we have chosen not to acknowledge him, even to the point of violating grammatical rules.

Dedication

In Special Tribute To Our Parents And Loved Ones Who Have Gone To Be With The Lord

    Martha Vassar Smith   Janice Rae Olmstead

    Earl Jesse Smith   Allen Lee Wolf

We do not want you to be uninformed, brothers and sisters, about those who have died, so that you may not grieve as others do who have no hope.

We believe that Jesus died and rose again, even so, through Jesus, God will bring with him those who have died.

For this we declare to you by the Word of the Lord, that we who are alive, who are left until the coming of the Lord.

For the Lord himself, with a cry of command, with the archangel's call and with the sound of God's trumpet will descend from Heaven, and the dead in Jesus Christ will rise first.

Then we who are alive, who are left, will be caught up in the clouds together with them to meet the Lord in the air; and so we will be with the Lord forever. (1Th.14.13-18)

We both had the distinct privilege of being born to Christian parents.

Thank you for feeding our spirits and for allowing us to feed yours.

You helped us to grow in untold ways.

Marsha and myself dedicate this book to your fond memories.

We salute the unending love you blessed us with.

Oscar & Marsha Smith
15 October 2011

Antonio & Tushekia,

God loves you! Your marriage has the potential to answer every question, solve every problem and satisfy the deep yearnings of your hearts.

Marsha and I love you —
Adotcomchurch.com
The family loves you!

Acknowledgements

I love You, O Lord, My strength. The Lord is my rock and my fortress
and my deliverer, My God, my rock, in whom I take refuge;
My shield and the horn of my salvation, my stronghold.
I call upon the Lord, who is worthy to be praised,
And I am saved from my enemies.
Psalm 18:1-3

Above all I want to thank my wife, Marsha, who supported and encouraged me in spite of all the time it took me to get this together and put it on paper. Without regard for her own needs and preferences, she has corrected my spelling, and helped me meet my deadlines. "Thank you" seems hardly sufficient to declare the depth of my gratitude.

I would like to thank my dear friend Ted Ciuba for enabling me to publish this book. Thank you for your unselfish commitment to and competent assistance in this rather involved project.

I would like to thank my sons Earl Jesse (EJ) and Henry Oscar Smith. Love you Alyssa our Niece who is attending her first day in Kindergarten.

Special Thanks to Charles Waters, Steve Galiher, Jeff Latour, Don Downs and Antonio Carter. AdotcomChurch.com is fully committed to creating synergy through strategic partnerships and we encourage your full support of our friends at theBridgeBunch.com where Pastor Bob is feeding over 4500 people a week right here in Nashville, TN.

My goal has been to ignite excitement about our Lord and Savior Jesus Christ. I make no apology about my everyday approach to critically important doctrines. This book is not for theologians, but for the truck driver, the athlete, the waitress, the high school student, the person in military service and the business person.

With God's help I want everyone who picks up this book to understand every word and grasp every principle. I freely confess, I want you to enjoy this book and to find out that discovering Scripture and seeing its importance can encourage you like nothing else. First and foremost it's always about the Word of God. The Local Church holds the hope of the world. There is hope for the future. There is forgiveness for the past. God and His Word are trustworthy. Jesus Christ is Our Savior. Jesus Christ is King. There is life -giving and life-changing truths found in God's Word. There is life-giving and life changing truths found in God's Word. As Mary stated at the wedding in Cana "whatsoever he tells you to do, do it". The spiritual destiny God has planned for us is based upon the one thing which can't be shaken and that is the infallible, impregnable Word of the living God. **Lord Jesus Christ Paid The Ultimate Price. We must look to Him and His leadership**. God has planned for us to be victorious and He is restoring divine order. He is coming in power and great glory to claim a bride that is pure, holy without spot or wrinkle. Now is God's time for the Church to get advanced knowledge through the Holy Spirit, to tap into the very mind of God and experience a supernatural manifestation taking us into the fullness of all that he has planned for us.

God's Servant,
Oscar Smith
Nashville TN
September 9, 2013

TABLE OF CONTENTS

Introduction	vii
Ch. 1: He Came Incognito	3
Ch. 2: We Give Our Thanks and All the Glory	9
Ch. 3: Let's Work Together to Restore	11
Ch. 4: Our Being in Christ is an Inheritance	13
Ch. 5: The Purchased Possession	17
Ch. 6: On Becoming a Prepared Vessel	23
Ch. 7: The Gracious Acts of God!	27
Ch. 8: The Changeless Promise	29
Ch. 9: The Stone Not Made With Hands	31
Ch. 10: Advancing the Significance of God	35
Ch. 11: The World Knew Him Not!	39
Ch. 12: Don't Be Afraid of Your Trial!	43
Ch. 13: Now Would Be a Good Time	49
Ch. 14: He Made Us Kings and Priests	55
Ch. 15: The Life That Wins	59
Ch. 16: Self-Inflicted Nonsense & Heavenly Vision	63
Ch. 17: Each of Us!	67
Ch. 18: The Believer Priest	71
Ch. 19: The Most Awesome Power of All	75
Ch. 20: How Excellent is Thy Name in All the Earth	79
Ch. 21: Stop Dancing With the Bear	83
Ch. 22: You Are Precious	87
Ch. 23: What a Privilege It Is	91
Ch. 24: Citizen of Heaven, Ambassador of God	93
Back Page Summary	111
Special Edition Message: Enjoy Life As God Intended	113
He Came Incognito Love	125
About the Author	139
About This Book	141

Introduction

"May the Holy Spirit take you beyond the limitations of your natural mind"

There are multiplied thousands of good books written about God. My desire here is not to just write a book to be read and placed on a shelf somewhere to gather dust. No, it is my prayer that as you read each page, regardless of your level of scholarship and or lack thereof, that you, yes *you*, will receive a new and all-consuming passion for the saving knowledge about Jesus Christ.

May the Holy Spirit take you beyond the limitations of your natural mind, as happened to me when I started hungering to learn more about who Jesus Christ truly is.

Some years ago, I had a Nashville-based radio show called Gratitude Life. This is the prayer that I made with my wife Marsha as we prepared our hearts to go on the air with the Gratitude Life Radio Ministry. We asked Him to open our spiritual understanding, and to teach us to pray prayers that touch God's heart. We asked Him to anoint our mouths with the fire of His Spirit. We asked him to release a new prayer anointing on us and our ministry. We asked Him to bring us into a new level of strategic warfare prayer, if you will. Beyond my understanding at the time, as a young Pastor, I began an exhaustive study of the resources of Jesus Christ in order to get some kind of measurement of the power that is that Name.

Ultimately, this book is a presentation of the power and authority vested in the name of Jesus Christ, and our Believer rights to use this name. My goal is to make the Word of God a living reality. The title *He Came Incognito* is appropriate, because He is that Name. All He was and all He did and all He will ever do is in that Name right now. He is healing right now. He is victory right now. He is our all-in-all right now.

At the time I began my radio ministry, I was actually sick and tired of sound bites and high-sounding phrase, and of quoting Scriptural sayings from memory—none of which had meaning to me inside my heart at all. Thank God for setting me aside for some intensive study, which I had to do to be cutting edge and relevant—not for the radio, but for my own deliverance from playing the Church game. We are what Jesus called "hearers of the Word, and not doers." The Finished Work of Jesus Christ has made a deposit for us in the Bank of Heaven that can't be overdrawn. We are heirs of God, joint heirs with Christ.

Thank you in advance for reading this book. I realize that many will say that it's a good read, and then put it down permanently. But you have a responsibility to help others understand what you will read in this book, and to never live a life of defeat ever again.

This message has been a struggle to put in writing, because I have been clinging to a historical Jesus who has been rendered powerless, unable to meet daily needs and heal the sick in the modern world. The miracle-working Jesus Christ has been ushered out of the Church with programs and entertainment. My wife and I almost feel uncomfortable around most Church folks, not knowing when we may be asked to leave because we *do* believe in supernatural miracle-working power today.

Seriously, what is the dominant thought in your Church today? A dead entertainment-focused Church has no resurrection power within it, no miracle-working force in back of it—it's just uneducated preachers leading the uneducated into thinking that miracles are not for today. But we need God's miraculous touch more than ever right now! Absolutely nothing but a return to the God of Miracles will save our land, our nation, and our world today.

Jesus Christ attracted the multitudes through miracles. People want Him. He is the same yesterday, today, and forever. Many of us have become purely five-senses driven, which develops our ego, pride, and selfishness. Church and prayer becomes a business proposition. But there is a deeper walk that is being shared in this book. It is of the first importance that we know what being a child of God really means. The Holy Spirit was given to us to be our guide, and to lead us into all truth. Love is a product of this Holy Spirit. Faith is a product of this Holy Spirit. Eternal life is a product of this Holy Spirit.

He Came Incognito is a revelation of the "hidden man of the heart" that we read about in 1 Peter 3:4. The only way to know God and Jesus Christ is through the Spirit. There are many who have heard the Word, and do not fully understand it. I have tried—and I'm certain you have too—to pick up the Bible and read and to comprehend what is being said; but understanding it is impossible without a historical perspective.

This Kingdom that Jesus came to bring is not earthly and geographical. The Kingdom is God's rule, and it is from Heaven that it originates, not Earth. God has always been sovereign. The message of Jesus Christ was that the Kingdom of God was "at hand." So there was an aspect of His reign that was arriving—which means that it had not arrived as of yet. Regardless of how it looks, though, the Kingdom is always advancing.

We may not understand or see it, but the Kingdom is always at work. The Kingdom is always growing. This Incognito Christ is not incognito to me any longer; and I trust you will come to this saving knowledge as well. The rule of Jesus Christ continues to advance from generation to generation.

Isaiah 9:7 says, "of the increase of His government and peace there will be no end," and look around; we are a global company of many millions.

Thank you for allowing an emotional introduction; but I just get excited when I think about how, when Jesus Christ was crucified, He took my place as a sinner. He bore my sins in His body on a tree for me; He bore my shame, which came through my union with Satan. He bore my diseases; He bore my judgments; He carried all this off to the Land of Forgetfulness, and he rose triumphantly, because He had put all this baggage away! In fact, He put Oscar Smith away, the old me—the sinner and my sinful nature as well. I stand today with Him and in Him as a FREE Man, as He was FREE when He rose.

Thank you for reading this book. God is waiting for you inside. Get ready to receive more about who Jesus Christ is, and how you can more fully experience Him in your life today.

He came incognito, but He is not incognito anymore!

He Came Incognito

How Jesus Christ is Relevant
to Your Life Today—and Always!

by

**Rev. Oscar Smith
Pastor, Gratitude Life
Nashville, Tennessee**

CHAPTER 1

He Came Incognito

Let's build with God's Spirit: (Malachi 2:16) "Take heed to your spirit."

All the deception—all the death and the dying in God's church—is more serious than anything else on earth. He carefully selected each one of His very elect to marry His Son. He is extremely cautious about who will marry His Son. We are The One Bride of Jesus Christ. We are The One, all to marry the Creator of the Universe!

God has to put us through test and trials; why? Because we are The One Bride! There will never be another! *We are The One.* Christ and God are totally involved in this relationship. Jesus Christ is coming to consummate the marriage covenant He made with us; but He is doing it differently than He did with ancient Israel. He is proving us first!

The Word, the Logos, a member of the Godhead, spilled His blood for us. Now He is offering the first fruits of His hand in marriage.

Per John 17:5: "And now, O Father, glorify thou me with thine own self with the glory which I had with thee before the world was." The word was with God! Philippians 2:5: "Let this mind be in you, which was also in Christ Jesus."

The Son never works of Himself, but always as the Revealer of the Father and the Executor of His Will. Jesus supported his Father and set an example for His Bride and for the world. As he tells us in John 14:9, "He that has seen me has seen the Father." Christ did not declare Himself; He declared His Father.

Behind closed doors, God, manifest your glory. God's candidness is awesome! He gives us a panoramic view: the total spectrum, not just the superficial. We need to see the total spectrum of what walking with God really looks like. When you say, "I'm blessed! I'm healed!" that is a one-dimensional testimony. How were you healed? How long did it take? How many scriptures did you quote?

God shared ordinary events, not just spectacular ones. The disciple's dilemma was God's unpredictable ways of doing things. Isolation brings revelation; strength is not perfected in crowds, in the spotlight. No, it is perfected in the shadows. Ministries of motives are perfected in weakness. Right reasons are discerned in the shadow. The Presence of God is our greatest weapon against the enemy. Consider these promises:

> "God will be an enemy to our enemies" (Exodus 23:22).
>
> "God will bless our daily provision" (Exodus 23:25).
>
> "God will take sickness from us" (Exodus 23:25).
>
> "God will prolong our days upon the earth" (Deuteronomy 4:40).
>
> "God will love, bless, and multiply us" (Deuteronomy 7:13).
>
> "We will possess the gate of our enemies" (Genesis 22:17).
>
> "We will prosper in all that we do" (Deuteronomy 29:9).
>
> "No good thing will God withhold from us" (Psalms 84:11).

We are in the midst of a special season; so today, July 26, 2011, I feel impressed of the Lord Jesus Christ to share this Prayer for Salvation with you. I encourage you to speak this prayer, and add your own name and date at the end:

> "Dear Father God, I realize that I have sinned against you, and that I can't SAVE myself. I believe that Jesus Christ died on the cross, and shed His blood to cleanse me from my sins. I believe that He rose from the grave that I might have Eternal Life. I ask You to forgive my sins and come into my life. I pray this sincerely. Amen!"

Name:

Date:

Our Prayer for Your Protection:

> "Dear Father God, please keep the one who just prayed this Prayer for salvation sincerely from their heart focused on You. Help them to know Your will for their life and to walk in all Your ways. Deliver them from all temptation, and help them to learn to honor and glorify You in all that they do. Thank You, Lord Jesus Christ, for all You have done for us. Amen and Amen."

Healing is a Process

I know how you feel: without relativity, you just have doctrine. Jesus said, "Don't pray like the Pharisees, trying to impress people." Enter in your secret closet—God pays you on the basis of what happens to you behind closed doors. Shut up with silent tears, Heaven hears your tears. Stop being impressive! God comes to you through the door; God does things behind closed doors. God told the widow woman to borrow empty vessels, bring them into the house, and shut the door. Shutting the door provokes the oils to flow behind closed doors. As long as there was an empty vessel, oil flowed.

Jarius told Jesus that his daughter was dead. Jesus shut the door and said *Te li ta cumi*: "Damsel, arise not publicly"—but privately, shut behind closed doors, Life returned to her. Lazarus was out of the view of people when he was revived. Revival happens behind closed doors when God says, "I'm not finished with you!"

Jesus was resurrected behind the closed door of his tomb. Jesus loosed Himself. Jesus spoke an outfit into existence, and walked out into the garden dressed; he left his grave clothes behind.

God assumes the responsibility of reincarnation. "Peace be with you" did not impress the disciples. We are dealing with a generation of people not easily impressed. Jesus came into His own leadership, and they were not impressed! He began to uncover His wounds! What we need is a "Believed Hero," not afraid to show their wounds, to expose their vulnerabilities. We need Clark Kent, not Superman. Put your cape in the closet, and give me a hero I can understand! Show me what you went through. Pain can make everybody relate.

The criterion for a Christian is to believe in the Lord, and you'll be saved. The criterion for a disciple is different. Discipleship requires a deeper level of commitment. You must pick up a cross and deny yourself. We're all walking with a cross on our back; be it marriage, family, finances, or whatever—somewhere there is a cross in your life. Everyone God uses has a cross, something you're nailed to as a child, a failure, a flaw, an occurrence. There is glory in the cross. Jesus had to expose his wounds; so the credentials behind our message is pain. It's our cross!

Being touched by someone else's infirmity leads to true ministry.

God	I'm	God says
we	bleeding	trust me!
glorify	but I'm	
you	trusting	

This is where we see the glory of the cross. Suffering leads to resurrection; you will come out of the secret closet with power. Impart life out of your pain! Show your wounds! We are a generation of warriors. Deliverance is in the house today; something good is coming out of this.

My ministry is to hurting people; that is where my job security comes from. Behind closed doors, folks are hurting; I help take them from hurting to a place of healing. Healing for your hurting places is in this house today. God wants to heal you today! You *will* see a change; this is for your wounds, the needs you nurse behind closed doors. God had to break you to bless you out of your pain; you *will* see gain.

Call out to him today, and God is going to renew your strength.

Lord, I bring these people—these crosses, spouses, children, broken promises— before you. Lay your hand here; breathe on this house right now; breathe into their broken, wounded places. Change their circumstances; bring restoration into this house today. I thank you, Master.

I speak to frustrations. I say, "Damsel, arise."

Folks planned funerals all around; God says, "Get up!"

God, give grace. Turn it around; a change is coming. Turn around in a circle in your home, and see God turning your situation around for us. Dance out of depression. Get your secret praise. Rejoice in the Lord today! Amen!

CHAPTER 2

We Give Our Thanks and All the Glory

to God

The message in this chapter is for folks involved in full-time Christian living! He came incognito in the person of Jesus of Nazareth: HE CAME INCOGNITO!

The Kingdom of God's Son

He is the Anointed One of God. The purpose of this King's coming to the world is to gather to Himself a people in whom, by the Spirit of God, he can build a Kingdom that is not of this world, but which is of Heaven. I want to speak this with care; this is the theme for this chapter!

The Gospel of Jesus Christ is The Gospel of the King. Jesus Christ is King and Lord of our very lives. Indeed, Jesus Christ is "the King of Kings and the Lord of Lords" (1 Timothy 6:15). We have to place ourselves daily under the kingship of Christ Jesus the Lord. He is the King set up by God...the King rejected by men. All God has done, He has done first of all to Christ our King.

We must surrender to the Lordship of Christ.

Jesus is our King; and as our King, He exposes the paradox of a divided heart. Matthew 6:24 tells us, "No one can serve two masters; for either he will hate the one and love the other, or he will be loyal to one and despise the other." Where is your allegiance today? Are you just giving lip service to loving God, or are you clinging to the love of this world system, the kingdom of this world?

One of the works of the Holy Spirit, as described by the Lord Jesus Himself, is to

"Bring to your remembrance all that I said unto you" (John 14:26).

Now Paul, in Colossians 3:16, says this regarding the Lord's Word: he calls it "the Word of Christ," rather than the "Word of God." The Word of God includes the whole Bible. The touch of our King/our Lord is powerful as He touches; His power counteracts our weakness!

Divine Truth is hidden from the wise and prudent, but is revealed to babes. The incarnation of God's Son was one of the greatest events in the history of the universe, and yet its actual occurrence was not made known to all of mankind. It was specifically revealed to the Bethlehem shepherds and wise men of the East! Indeed, Jesus Christ our King is not made known to all even today.

God is sovereign. Look at who He made known the birth of a "Savior," to illustrate shepherds and heathens from a far country. They were singled out for this Divine Honor.

CHAPTER 3

Let's Work Together to Restore

an Attitude of Gratitude

We believe there is a Godly remnant who will say, "Thank you, Jesus Christ. Thank you Lord, thank you King of Kings! We believe in the Sovereign exercise of Grace! Grace reins through righteousness. Divine Grace, Divine Sovereignty, and Divine Truth— Sovereign Truth."

We must learn this basic truth: that the Creator is our absolute sovereign. Proverbs 16:4 reminds us: "The Lord has made all things for Himself." So whom will you serve? He is the Creator, the Governor, the King of Kings; and His Kingdom rules over all (Psalms 103:19). That's why pride is so dangerous. There seems to me to be a lusting for titles of authority today. It's a prideful lusting: Bishop, Apostle, Doctor, Elder, Chairman, etc. Over many years, I have seen how dangerous titles can become.

Jesus Christ is our King. Why not be happy taking the position of serving Him? Let's turn our eyes back toward giving Him all the thanks and all the glory. Let us together work to restore an Attitude of Gratitude to the Lord.

Jesus draws us into His presence not that we should replace Him, or even develop equality with Him, but that we may worship and adore Him. We need to thank Him today for His tender love. Let us give thanks to God right now out of a heart full of love. After all, everything we obtain comes to us through His mercy and grace.

I trust you will stop trying to convince the world that Christianity is true because Jesus makes us thinner, prettier, wealthier, more successful, more popular, stronger, and more influential. This is what we truly need to share with others: Our pride wants instant results, but our God is in no hurry. We have to be very careful when we grasp at the promises and blessings of God, lest we lose the presence for the lust of the Loaves and Fishes! "No eye has seen, no ear has heard, no mind has conceived what God has prepared for those who love Him" (1 Corinthians 2:9).

The word pride is spelled with a big "I" in the middle. Think of it as an acronym, Please Realize I Deserve Exaltation, P-R-I-D-E. Pride is the most deceptive of sins. In Proverbs 8:13, God says that He hates pride, and warns in Proverbs 16:18, "Pride goes before destruction, and an haughty spirit before a fall." This thing called pride is too big for us to handle alone. It will outthink, outsmart, and outmaneuver each of us, each and every time.

He came into this world incognito! Jesus Christ was God's perfect model of humility. There was no pride in Him. Put off pride; put *on* Christ!

The Question of the Day?

Romans 2:4 asks, "Or despise you the riches of His goodness?" The truth is, God's goodness *is* despised today. However as Psalm 52:1 teaches, "The goodness of God endures continually." God is absolutely perfect; nothing about God is defective, and absolutely nothing can be added to make God any better! He is not only good, but goodness itself. He is the Highest Good. "The Lord is good to all: and his tender mercies are over all his works" (Psalm 145:9).

"Oh that men would praise the Lord for His goodness, and His wonderful works to the children of men!" (Psalm 107:8).

"The Lord is good, a stronghold in the day of trouble, and He knows them that trust Him" (Nahum 1:7).

CHAPTER 4

Our Being in Christ is an Inheritance

Truly, our being in Christ really is an inheritance; all we have to do is to receive and enjoy it. God has accomplished everything in Christ. That's why the scriptural passage 1 Corinthians 1:30 is so very, very precious: "But of Him, you are in Christ Jesus." God has put us in Christ! This is an inheritance we can enjoy! God has made Christ our righteousness, our sanctification, and our redemption.

Joy is *not* when we are happy. Joy is Christ living within us, and being expressed as joy. We have to see that nothing from ourselves will satisfy His heart; everything must

be of Him. He has accomplished everything. His life is ours. His facts are ours. His experiences are ours—and His power is ours! God is the source, and Christ is the one he is working through.

From the beginning to the end, it is all a matter of receiving God's grace. There are two aspects of grace; there are two aspects of the inheritance God has given to us in Christ. 1. We are in Christ. 2. Christ is in us.

John 15:4-5 reminds us, "Abide in me and I in you ...he who abides in Me and I in him." We have to realize that all of God's provisions in Christ are our inheritance. We have to know Christ in these two aspects! If we only know that we are in Christ, we will be weak and empty. If we only know that Christ is in us, without knowing that we are in Christ, we will suffer a great deal. Together, these two aspects of grace will deliver us from our own work and self-effort. He offers us a new start, a new standing, a new beginning. God pulled us out of the mire and set our feet on the rocks...and we go forward from there!

Gratitude

We talked about the life that wins. When we die, everything is FINISHED! It's finished. Finito! If we want to have a new start before God, we need a new life. But a new life is not enough! We still need a new position.

With our Adamic life in us, we did not become wicked after we did something wrong; we were wicked as soon as we were born! We inherited a wrong life. This is what the first three chapters of Romans shows us: that our conduct is wrong. Chapters 5-8 show us our *person* is wrong. Per Romans 6:7, "for he that is dead is freed from sin."

But if we be dead with Christ, we must believe that we also live with him. Everything in Adam is terminated, and now we can have a new beginning

Gratitude: thank and praise the Lord. He has joined us in Christ, as we learn in 1 Corinthians 1:30: "But of Him you are in Christ Jesus." God accomplished our: Co-Death, Co-Resurrection, and Co-Ascension with Christ.

Now, God's Word does not say that we should be crucified. It says, "I *have* been crucified." You and I and Christ are Joined Together. This reality, this truth, must become our inheritance. It's God's inheritance to us in Christ. We must receive grace from God to realize that we can't initiate anything! We are not worthy of initiating anything! Genesis 1 begins, "In the beginning, God created the Heavens and the Earth." It's all about God—not us! God is the Father, and *everything* originates from Him.

It is a day of gratitude, the day that God shows you that He is the Father. God wants us as His children, His sons and daughters. He is the one Who "calls us out." God, You are my source. Everything depends on You. You are the Initiator of Everything. "Behold what manner of love the Father has bestowed upon us, that we should be called the sons of God: therefore the world knows us not, because it knew him not" (1 John 3:1).

I had to sit back and think very deeply about this! If you and I are sons of the Father, then that makes us family. Where will you go with this reality today? The world knows us not!

The unveiling of His plan officially began with the birth of Jesus Christ. It will involve all humans who submit to Almighty God. Look at 1 John 3:2: "Beloved, now we are the sons of God and it does not appear what we shall be: but we know that, when He shall appear, we shall be

Our Being in Christ is an Inheritance

like Him; for we shall see Him as He is." The Father's vision of family shows us the depth of the Father's love for man, as seen in John 3:16.

Jesus Christ was the only son who could make it possible for the Father to have many more sons. Isaiah 9:6-7 shows us that God has placed His government upon Christ's shoulder. God gave the world a Son. That means family. With His Son, He established His government!

Abraham is known as the father of the faithful. He had real faith in a real vision.

Abraham obeyed God. In Hebrews 11:8-10, Paul tells us that by faith, Abraham looked for a city which had foundations—sure foundations. And that is what our faith should be built and established upon. Sure foundations, whose builder and maker is God!

Jesus Christ came with one message. "Jesus began to preach, and to say, Repent: for the Kingdom of Heaven is at hand" (Matthew 4:17). That was the good news: the family vision, the family of God, the government of God. The Kingdom of God. God paid a great price to give us this vision of the future. He allowed His Son to be crucified so that all humans could be part of the future spiritual family!

God gave Abraham the experience of knowing God as his Father. God showed Abraham that everything comes from God!

Abraham, Isaac and Jacob are the beginning of the history of God's people. The Bible says we are fellow citizens and members of the household of God (Ephesians 2:19). Furthermore, Jesus said that we would see Abraham, Isaac and Jacob "in the Kingdom of God" (Luke 13:28). And that "many will come from the East and the West and will recline at the table with Abraham, Isaac and Jacob in the Kingdom of the Heavens" (Matthew 8:11).

In Abraham, we see God's purpose. In Isaac, we see God's power. In Jacob, we see God's progress. In the Kingdom of God, we are members of the Royal Family.

How real is this family vision to you? The family vision is what Salvation is all about! Jesus was crucified for bringing this message. We are citizens by inheritance in the Father's Royal Family Kingdom!

CHAPTER 5

The Purchased Possession

The Kingdom of Heaven is the Purchased Possession! (Ephesians 1:14).

This is a "purchased possession" for His people by the whole redemptive work of Christ. His precious blood gives every believer and every believing sinner the legal right to enter the holiest place (Hebrews 10:19). Our title to glory is found alone in Christ.

Christ not only delivers us from death, but he purchased life for us! He not only put away our sins, but merited an inheritance for us!

"Giving thanks unto the Father who has made us meet to be partakers of the inheritance of the saints in light, Who has delivered us from the power of darkness, and has translated us into the Kingdom of His dear Son: In whom we have redemption through His blood, even the forgiveness of sins." This is Paul the Apostle speaking in Colossians 1:12-14.

Now let's look at Obadiah 17: "But upon Mt. Zion shall be deliverance, and there shall be holiness, and the house of Jacob shall possess their possessions." Mt. Zion: that is what God's church is called!

Let's go back to Colossians 1:12. Let's note that Heaven is here termed an "inheritance," as I discussed in the last chapter. An inheritance is not purchased by our own labors or good works! We lawfully succeed to an inheritance by virtue of our relationship to another. The son or daughter receives or succeeds by virtue of his or her relationship to their father or mother, aunt or uncle. The son of a king inherits the crown. In the case that Paul is presenting, this inheritance is given over by virtue of being sons and daughters of God! We are joint heirs with Christ!

Colossians 1:13 tells us we have been translated into the Kingdom of His dear son Jesus Christ. Similarly, Revelation 1:5 says that already He has made us "kings and priests unto God." And what is the inheritance of a king?

- A crown
- A throne
- A kingdom

Consider Romans 5:17. Let's look at the "B" side of this verse: "...much more they which receive abundance of grace and of the gift of righteousness shall reign in life by one, Jesus Christ." This is what we are sharing and identifying as "the Purchased Possession!" We sit with Him on His throne to reign with Him forever! That is the dignity of our inheritance! We are joint heirs; our destiny is bound up with the destiny of our Lord, our King Jesus Christ!

We have to rise above the messenger and get excited about the message that the Kingdom of Heaven is the "Purchased Possession" of Jesus Christ. Our title to the inheritance is the righteousness of Christ. Our challenge is to surrender 100% to the Lordship and the Kingship of Jesus Christ. We have to resolve to be ruled by Jesus our King. Everything God does for his people is for Christ's sake.

Let's look at Ephesians 1:6: "To the praise of the story of His grace, wherein he has made us accepted in the beloved." There can be no real progress without a better acquaintance with His person, His office and His works. To receive our "Purchased Possession," we have to surrender to the authority of Jesus Christ and receive Him as a king who reigns over our hearts and our lives. Let's look at Jude 1:21: "Keep yourselves in the love of God, looking for the mercy of our Lord Jesus Christ to eternal life."

The Holy Spirit Had Me to Look at the Eagle

Remember, scripture says: "come out of her, my people" (Revelation 18:4). The "come out" refers to anything that would hinder your walk with God.

As a "purchased possession," let us look at the Eagle.

Eagles fly alone at high altitude, and do not mix with sparrows or smaller birds. Birds of a feather flock together. No other bird goes to the height of the eagle. Eagles fly with eagles, though never in a flock. Even when Moses of the Old Testament went to commune with God on the mountain, he left the crowd at the foothills. Stay away from sparrows and ravens. Eagles fly with eagles.

Eagles have strong vision, which focuses up to five kilometers (three miles) away. When an eagle sights prey—even a rodent—from this distance, he narrows his focus on it and sets out to get it. No matter the obstacle, the eagle will not move his focus from the prey until he grabs it. So have a vision and remain focused, no matter what the obstacle, and you will succeed.

Eagles do not eat dead things; they feed on fresh prey. Vultures eat dead animals, not eagles. So steer clear of outdated and old information. Do your research, always.

The eagle is the only bird that loves the storm. When clouds gather, the eagle gets excited. The eagle uses the winds of the storm to rise, and is pushed up higher. Once it finds the wind of the storm, the eagle stops flapping and uses the pressure of the raging storm to glide and soar through the clouds. This gives the eagle an opportunity to rest its wings. In the meantime, all the other birds hide in the leaves and branches of the trees. We can use the storms of our lives (obstacles, trouble, etc.) to rise to greater heights. Achievers relish challenges, and use them profitably. Keep in mind that the eagle is the only bird that rises above the storm to soar in the heavens until the storm passes. They do this because the eagle is the only bird God created with the ability to lock its wings in a fixed position, which enables it to be at rest as it soars high above the storm clouds.

The eagle tests before it trusts. When a female eagle meets a male, she flies down to Earth with the male pursuing her and she picks a twig. She flies back into the air with the male pursuing her. Once she has reached a height high enough for her, she lets the twig fall to the ground and watches it as it falls. The male chases after the twig. The faster it falls, the faster he chases it, until he reaches it and has to catch it before it hits the ground. Then he brings it back to the female eagle. The female eagle grabs the twig and flies to a much higher altitude, pursued by the male, until she perceives it is high enough; and then she drops the twig for the male to chase. This goes on for hours, with the height increasing until the female eagle is assured that the male eagle has mastered the art of picking the twig, which shows commitment; then, and only then, will she allow him to mate with her! So whether in private life or in business, one should test the commitment of people intended for partnership.

Eagles prepare for training. When the female is about to lay eggs, the female and male eagle identify a place very high on a cliff, then the male flies to Earth again to collect twigs, which he lays in the intended nest. He flies back to Earth and picks thorns, and lays them on top of the twigs. He flies back to Earth and picks soft grass to cover the thorns, and then flies back to pick rugs to put on the grass. When this first layering is complete the male eagle runs back to earth and picks more thorns, lays them on the nest; runs back to get grass and rugs and lays them on top of the thorns; then plucks his feathers to complete the nest. The thorns on the outside of the nest protect it from possible intruders. Both male and female eagles participate in raising the eagle family. She lays the eggs and protects them; he builds the nest and hunts.

When training the young ones to fly, the male eagle throws the eaglets out of the nest; and because they are scared, they jump into the nest again. Next, the female throws them out and then takes off the soft layers of the nest, leaving the thorns bare. When the scared eaglets jump into the nest again, they're pricked by thorns. Shrieking and bleeding, they jump out again, this time wondering why the mother and father who love them so much are torturing them. Next, mother eagle pushes them off the cliff into the air.

As they shriek in fear, father eagle flies out and picks them up on his back before they fall, and brings them back to the cliff. This goes on for some time, until they start flapping their wings. They get excited at this newfound knowledge that they can fly and not fall at such a fast rate. The father and mother eagle support them with their wings. The preparation of the nest teaches us to prepare for changes; the preparation for the family teaches us that active participation of both partners leads to success; being pricked by the thorns tells us that sometimes being too comfortable where we are may result into our not experiencing life, not progressing, and not learning at all. The thorns of life teach us that we need to grow, get out of the nest, and live on. We may not know it, but the seemingly comfortable and safe haven may have thorns. The people who love us do not let us languish in sloth, but push us hard to grow and prosper. Even in their seemingly bad actions, they have good intentions for us.

When the eagle grows old, his feathers become weak and cannot take him as fast as they should. When he feels weak and about to die, he retires to a place far away in the rocks. While there, he plucks out every feather on his body until he is completely bare. He stays in this hiding place until he has grown new feathers; then he can come out. We occasionally need to shed bad habits and items that burden us without adding to our lives.

On the cross, we see a divinely ordained exchange that took place, which was conceived in God's heart and mind from eternity and acted out at Calvary. The Cross was no accident, and it was no mishap forced on Jesus Christ. By this one sacrifice, He made provision for all the needs of the whole human race in every area of our lives, for time and for eternity. All the evil due to us came on Jesus Christ, and all the good due Jesus Christ due to His sinless obedience was made available to us.

Isaiah 53:4-5: "Surely He has borne our griefs, and carried our sorrows; yet we did esteem Him stricken, smitten of God, and afflicted. But he was wounded for our transgressions, He was bruised for our iniquities: the chastisement of our peace was upon Him; and with His stripes we are healed."

This Divinely Ordained Exchange actually can be better called the Eight Exchanges:

1. His punishment for our forgiveness.

2. His wounding for our healing.

3. His righteousness in place of sin.

4. His life in place of death.

5. His blessings in place of poverty.

6. His abundance in place of shame.

7. His acceptance in place of rejection.

8. The new man in place of the old man.

The ongoing outworking of what He did on the cross is our Salvation.

I have found that one of the most practical ways to appropriate what God has done for me is to thank Him for it. So I confess with my mouth:

> "Jesus Christ was punished that Oscar Smith may be forgiven. Jesus Christ was wounded that Oscar Smith might be healed. Lord Jesus Christ, Oscar Smith says thanks, because today I have peace with God through you."

Once our sin has been dealt with in God's way, the result is peace with God. Colossians 1:19-22 really makes plain this truth that I'm trying to share: "For it pleased the Father that in Him should all fullness dwell...by Him to reconcile all things to Himself; by Him...whether things on earth, or things in Heaven, having made peace through the blood on the cross. And you who once were alienated and enemies in your mind by wicked works, yet now He has reconciled in the body of His flesh through death, to present you holy and blameless and above reproach in His sight."

He came incognito, and He became totally identified with everything evil that any man, woman or child ever did; therefore, it is now possible for us to be forgiven and delivered from the power of evil. Another powerful Scripture that helps me bring this point home in Ephesians 1:7: "In Jesus Christ we have redemption through His blood, the forgiveness of sins, according to the riches of His grace."

When we have forgiveness of sins, we have redemption. The word "redemption" means to buy back, or to ransom. Through the price of the blood of Jesus Christ given on our behalf as a sacrifice, we now have been bought back from Satan to God.

CHAPTER 6

On Becoming a Prepared Vessel

In the Gospel, we find that whenever men came to our Lord Jesus Christ, He always had the right word. Our Lord's words were most appropriate, for he knew all men. What Jesus said was always right to the point. No doctor can use the same prescription for all his or her patients. In every diagnosis, you must have certainty.

Sometimes we may discover that a particular trouble is beyond our ability to help. If we have not first been a partaker of spiritual understanding, how can we hope to help the rest of God's children? The prayer is: "Oh Lord, do not let me go untouched, unbroken and unprepared."

We must pass through God's dealings, on becoming a prepared vessel!

The starting point of a spiritual work is marked by many re-adjustments made before God. It takes many breakings in many, many areas of our lives for us to attain a place of usefulness. The one who has accepted the most discipline is the one who can serve the best. The more one is broken, the more sensitive one becomes. The more loss one has suffered, the more he has to give.

Whenever we preserve or excuse ourselves at that point, we are deprived of spiritual sensitivity and supply. One who has learned can serve. Any delay in learning means a delay in serving. The way of service lies in brokenness! In 100% acceptance of the discipline of the Holy Spirit, emotions and cleverness will not help. The more we learn, the more we discern.

Only as we have experienced the Lord's strict dealing with us in a certain matter can we quickly detect even the initial sprouting in others. We do not need to wait for its fruit! We can discern it long before harvest time. Our spiritual sensitivity is gradually gained through experiencing God's hand upon us. And this is the only way of becoming a prepared vessel.

Paul states in 2 Corinthians 5:16: "We henceforth know no man according to flesh"—but according to spirit! Spirit is revealed. Real intentions are revealed. Always pay careful attention to the spirit's condition; issues of the heart, not just the words! Matthew 12:34 says, "Out of the abundance of the heart, the mouth speaks."

God is at work in our lives, unceasingly! Many years of sufferings, trials, temptations, hindrances, and disappointments; I now know this is the hand of God, daily seeking to carry on his work of preparing me to become a "prepared vessel." It is not easy, nor did I ever think it would be easy! There are endless rounds of difficulty!

Today, as I sit waiting and enjoying the peace and the presence of the Almighty God, I praise the Lord for the work of grace in my life.

Psalms 62:5-8 instructs: "My soul, wait thou only upon God, for my expectation is from Him. He only is my rock and my salvation: He is my defense; I shall not be moved. In God is my salvation and my glory; the rock of my strength, and my refuge, is in God. Trust in Him at all times; ye people, pour out your heart before Him: God is a refuge for us. Amen."

Life must be brought through the darkness and death of its own ability. Self-ability! Jesus Christ has planned that we should find rest unto our souls by way of His yoke. Paul says in 2 Corinthians 4:16-18, "For which cause we faint not, but though our outward man perish, yet the inward man is renewed day by day. For our light affliction, which is not for a moment, works for us a far more exceeding and eternal weight of glory; While we look not at the things which are seen, but at the things which are not seen: for the things which are seen are temporal; but the things which are not seen are eternal."

In becoming a prepared vessel, it is imperative that my outward life be replaced and the inner—inward life come forth. My willingness to serve God and my outward desires were not at all in harmony when God called me into his service. I did not want to come under nor submit to the Holy Spirit's control, which made me incapable of obeying God's call on my life. Brokenness was necessary. The alabaster box in my life had to be broken.

On Becoming a Prepared Vessel

My question for you is, are you still treasuring your alabaster box? Do you think your outward man is more precious because of success, wealth, possessions, your salt worth, your self-esteem? Are you treasuring your cleverness? Are you treasuring your importance? Are you treasuring your eloquence? Are you treasuring your superiority?

On becoming a prepared vessel—without the breaking of the outward, the inward will not come forth! The question is, are you containing or releasing the fragrance?

Each trial, each disciplinary working of the Holy Spirit, has but one purpose: to break our outward man so that our inward man may come through. Sufferings, challenges, testings; the Lord is preparing a way to use us.

The treasure is in the earthen vessel. Brokenness is the way of blessing, the way of fruitfulness. The Lord has not wasted even one experience in our lives. Troubles and testings are for our highest good. Our greatest trials are for our greatest profit!

CHAPTER 7

The Gracious Acts of God!

God declares all who believe in Jesus Christ as Lord, Jesus Christ as King, to be righteous! Please pay close attention to what is being said.

Justification is the gracious act of God, in declaring righteous the sinner who believes in Jesus Christ. Justification is an act, not a process! No Christian is more justified than any other Christian! Instantly, the believer is given a righteous standing before God. It is the gracious act of God.

Now let me say this: justification is unchanging! Justification gives us a new standing before God, just as even a newborn baby has a legal standing before the law. Justification settles things permanently, eternally. Justification means not only that God forgets our sins past, present, and future, but that God forgets we were ever sinners!

Let me break this down for you. Let me share with you a great illustration of justification. When I was growing up, the father of a buddy of mine owned a Rolls Royce. While out driving the car, it broke down; and so he called the dealership, saying, "I'm having trouble, what do you suggest?" Well, Rolls Royce sent out a mechanic who immediately fixed the car. As you can imagine, he was saying, "What is this going to cost me?" So once he got home, he wrote a nice letter thanking the mechanic and asking the dealership how much he owed them. He received a letter that read, "Dear Sir: There is no record anywhere in our files that anything ever went wrong with a Rolls Royce!"

The devil accuses you, and you accuse yourself; but God checks the files and says, "There is no record anywhere that my child ever did anything wrong." *That's* justification!

Now, let us look at "the dying robber, the saved thief." In the solution of the dying thief, we have a clear view of victorious grace such as is to be found nowhere else in the Bible! God is the God of all grace; salvation is entirely by His grace. According to Ephesians 2:8, by grace are we saved. Grace planned salvation, grace provided salvation, grace begins, grace continues, grace consummates our salvation. The dying thief...well, he had no moral character. He did not respect the law of man or God. He had no good works.

It is highly probable that as one who followed the occupation of a thief, this was the first time he saw Jesus Christ. Out of the heart of God comes the SOLUTION to the human problem. Jesus Christ says "Here am I, send Me." The disciples had no way to know that Jesus was going to be made Sin on the cross. They did not know He was going to die spiritually. They did not know that it was He who would be their Substitute. They did not know He was going to put Sin away, and make it possible for us to legally receive Eternal Life, the very nature of God!

They did not know that the Man of the Cross was going to rise again from the dead, and was going to be the Head of a New Creation.

They did not know that Eternal Life was a revolutionary experience.

They did not know where Jesus Christ had gone when His body was pronounced dead on the cross.

They did not know he was going to become the new High Priest.

Now, just take a good look at Psalm 22, which gives us a graphic picture of the crucifixion of Jesus Christ. This is more vivid than the accounts of John, Matthew, or Mark, who witnessed it. He came incognito to be the Father Pleaser. Every other man had lived to please himself. At last, God has a Man on Earth that lives to do His Will.

Chapter 8

The Changeless Promise

God has sworn by oath to Himself to make of this creation "Sons" in the image and likeness of God. This was a changeless promise. Abraham was made the beneficiary of these promises.

Let's read Galatians 3:15: "Brethren, I speak in the manner of men: though it is only a man's covenant, yet if it is confirmed, no one annuls or adds to it." And Hebrews 9:17: "For a testament is in force after men are dead, since it has no power at all while the testator lives."
Now let's look back at Galatians 3:16: "Now to Abraham and his seed were the promises made. He does not say And to seeds, as of many; but as one, And to your seed, who is Christ."

This was a changeless promise. This is a spiritual promise; that is, it is a promise meant to be fulfilled in Christ, in the spiritual seed. Galatians 3:19-20: "What purpose then does the law serve? It was added because of transgressions, till the seed should come to whom the promise was made: and it was appointed through angels by the hand of a mediator. Now a mediator does not mediate for only one, but God is one."

In addition to the law being a mediator, it was also a tutor to bring us to Christ, that we might be justified by faith. And as Galatians 3:26 points out, "For you are all Sons of God through faith in Christ Jesus." The changeless promise gives us the grace of Sonship. The law never creates Sons! The promise of Sonship was meant to be fulfilled through Abraham's seed: one, not many! We are Sons of the living God. We are the roots of the living God. Sonship was never the promise of the law!

Our connection to Abraham is through Christ. This promise was never meant to be for Abraham's natural children, but to be followed through Abraham's one seed—the Christ. We are, after all, the body of which Jesus Christ is the head. The head is seated in Heaven. The body is in the Earth. The anointing is on our head; the oil has been poured upon the head, and it runs down upon the body. We're the body in the same way that a body is absolutely ruled and governed by a head. That's why we say that we are citizens of God's Kingdom. We live in the Earth to give Christ our King a place and the physical means to do what he wants us to do. As the body of Christ, we commit to His purposes.

Now let's break this down by reading Isaiah 42:8: "I am the Lord, that is my name! I will not give my glory to another or my praise to idols!"

Brothers and sisters who have been following my ministry for some time know that we have been preaching that there is a counterfeit gospel being preached! So in Isaiah our God says, "I will not give my glory to another!" But we are not the "another" that is being referred to here. We are the body of Christ, elected to preach the only message that Christ came to preach. "But seek you first His kingdom and His righteousness" (Matthew 6:33). What doctrine, what gospel are you following? Jesus only came with one! The changeless promise makes us Sons and Heirs according to the promise. And Sonship has its privileges!

1. Being clothed in the glory of God.

2. Resting in His provisions.

3. Resting in His protection.

4. Being raised in the character of God.

5. Being trained to walk in maturity as a Son of God

CHAPTER 9

The Stone Not Made With Hands

"Jesus said: My kingdom is not of this world!" (John 18:36). What does this mean, not of this world? There is a Kingdom that belongs to our Lord Jesus Christ. Moreover, it is this Kingdom that displaces this world and the Earth! When the "stone not made with hands" shatters man's proud-prideful image, then the kingdom of this world will become the kingdom of our Lord and of His Christ.

God can set us upon a "rock" and keep our feet from slipping.

Everything our King says matters, and he means what he says! What the Lord our King says must stand—and we need to pay attention to what is being said. We know that every good gift that God offers to us is given to meet a contrasting evil! He gives us eternal life because there is death. He offers us forgiveness because there are sins. He gives us justification because there is condemnation, and he gives us salvation to deliver us from this world system.

Salvation is a God-ordered system. Let me repeat this: *Salvation is a God-ordered system* that brings us into His Kingdom, and under His spiritual authority. We are saved now out of a system constructed in defiance of the Purpose of God. Salvation means I make an act from the patterns of the world. I set my heart upon the things God's heart is set upon! I step out of "that" and I step into "this." When you are saved, you publicly declare that you belong to another system of things. Jesus Christ is now your Lord and your King!

We are saved through the resurrection of Jesus Christ. God has set His Son supreme above everything. There are two worlds: the Adamic world, and the new creation in Christ's world. We are born into the Adamic race, and we enter into the Kingdom of God by birth as well!

Our Adamic race history has been concluded in the death of Christ. So when you walk away from that burial, that funeral, you can say that you are a "finished man" or "finished woman." You now serve the "lifted up" Son of God: Jesus Christ, King of Kings. Lord of Lords.

When God comes to us with the revelation and the true understanding of the "finished work of Christ," he not only shows us ourselves there on the cross; he shows us our world there too! Everything that stirs pride in us is of this world. And what did we say about pride? It stands for Please Recognize "I" Desire Exaltation!

Every glory that is not glory to God is vainglory. At Gratitude Life we give all honor and thanks to our Lord, Savior and King, Jesus Christ, Son of God. Paul says: "Far be it from me to glory save in the cross of our Lord Jesus Christ, through which the world has been crucified with me, and I unto the world" (Galatians 6:14).

Time to break it down. Time to make it plain.

True transformation into the Kingdom of God is illustrated in Luke 19. Basically, Jesus says to Zaccheus (Zack): "You are very good with money. Don't stop being good with money, but do it now with different principles." Zack accepts Jesus Christ and salvation comes to his house, which in those days meant his business as well! Zack personally accepted Christ and also accepted Christ into his business.

May I now direct your attention to words Jesus said to the Jews in John 8:23: "You are from beneath; I am from above: you are of this world; I am not of this world." He was telling them outright, "Your place of origin is beneath; my place of origin is above." Origin determines everything!

This is reflected when Jesus turns to his disciples and says, "If you were of this world, the world would love its own: but because you are not of this world, but I chose you out of the world, therefore the world hates you" (John 15:19). We too, brothers and sisters in Christ, have been "chosen out" of this world. Thence comes the Church of Gratitude, Gratitude Life—the "Ekklesia," God's "called-out ones!" One here, one there; a call from God is a call *out of* the world.

This is our privilege. "Go you into all the world and preach the gospel" (Mark 16:15). Plumbers, bricklayers, truck drivers, technicians, medical personnel, business owners, car salespeople, lawyers—these are our mission fields! These are the areas where we should be! Everything we do—shop, factory, kitchen, hospital or school—has spiritual value in terms of the Kingdom of God. Everything is to be claimed for Him. Nowhere in scripture does it tell us concerning sin that we are to "overcome it," but it distinctly says we are to "overcome" the world.

In relation to sin, God's word speaks only of deliverance; it is in relation to the world that it speaks of victory. Be of good cheer. Be thankful. "I have overcome the world" (John 16:33). "The Prince of this world comes, and has nothing in me" (John 14:30).

"As thou did send me into the world, even so I send them into the world" (John 17:18). What a statement! We've been "planted" in the world, right in the midst of empty dust territory! (Genesis 1:26). It's a colony of Heaven. A divine settlement—an alien intrusion called the children of God. The Kingdom of God—the righteousness, peace, and joy people.

Paul says we are in the midst of a crooked and perverse generation, among whom we are seen as lights in the world (Philippians 2:15). God has deliberately placed us here; we are to expose our divine light for all men to see. We are to proclaim to men the good news that, if they will turn to it, that light of God in the face of Jesus Christ will set them free from the world's vanity. It will turn empty dust into the fullness of divine life.

Empty Dust Versus Divine Life

As children of God, we have a vital place in the world. We are called to overcome the world, not to run and hide from the world system! We must accept with joy the fact that God has placed us in the world. When the dust settles, we will walk out alive—alive in Christ.

Without any fear of challenge, Jesus our King could say, "I am the light of the world" (John 8:12). In Matthew 5:14 He says to His disciples, "You are the light of the world." Well, let me take my time and say it this way: we do not have to try to be the light of this world—we *are* the world's light! The divine life planted in us is our light source! That divine life is something the world can't give you; it is joy, peace, and love! (Galatians 5:22).

He said it, and He overcame it! And because he said it, we dare now say it too.

Because whosoever is begotten of God overcomes the world. Say it aloud: "I can be in the same world my Lord was in, and in the same sense as He was, I can be apart from it." You can be "as a lamp set on a lamp stand, giving light to all who enter the house. As He is, so are we in this world" (1 John 4:17).

Will you glorify God by radiating His light in this world? This is the place to glorify God. Give Him thanks today!

Chapter 10

Advancing the Significance of God

Advancing the significance of God, advancing the significance of Jesus Christ, advancing His significant cause, accepting His secured significance as sufficient—all this is critical! Surrendering our lives to His glory, surrendering our lives to His gain! To God alone be all the glory. Christ and Christ alone is preeminent. He is the only truly significant person in the universe. He deserves our commitment to reflect His significance, not our own.

In Colossians 1:13-16, Paul shared with us the ultimate, unsurpassed significance of Christ: "For God has rescued us from the dominion of darkness and brought us into the Kingdom of the Son He loves, in whom we have redemption, the forgiveness of sins. He is the image of the invisible God, the firstborn over all creation. For by Him all things were created: things in Heaven and on Earth, visible and invisible, whether thrones or powers, or rulers or authorities; all things were created by Him and for Him!"

John the Baptist said, "He must increase, but I must decrease" (John 3:30).

Satan was able to begin the fall of the human race by telling Eve that she was not quite significant enough! He offered her the added significance of being like God, and she accepted it! She and Adam turned their backs on "secured significance." The seduction of significance is very powerful! Adam and Eve lacked nothing, yet they doubted whether or not they had enough.

Our world is full of seductive lures to significance. But Jesus Christ says, "I am the way and the truth and the life. No one comes to the Father except through me" (John 14:6).

Redemption is a wonderful reality! God has taken the initiative to walk back into the Garden of Eden, looking for Adam and Eve. In mercy and in grace, He sought them out! We need to be grateful; we need to be filled with gratitude for God's restoring love and mercy. Our significance is fully secured, it is fully restored. We are now able to serve for Christ's glory and the advancing of His Kingdom. We are joint heirs with Christ (Romans 8:16-17). We are now Kingdom citizens!

In John 17:15-17, Christ prayed not that his Father would take us out of this world, but set us apart in the world by our commitment to the truth! We now live by the standards of the Kingdom to which we belong, the Kingdom of Christ! Per Matthew 9:17. "We now pour new wine into new wineskins." This is the reality of our new Kingdom—that you and I need to adopt new objectives of Kingdom living daily, with new resolve. We must learn to re-direct our inner energies of pleasure, pride, and passion.

Magnifying the significance of Christ does involve a loss of independent identity! We can no longer boast about being self-made, self-managed. We must become Christ-made people, people who proudly and gladly give Him all the credit and all the glory! We must let God become credible to a world that considers Him incredible.

"May God be gracious to us, and bless us and make His face shine upon us. That your ways be known on Earth, and your salvation among all nations. May the people praise you, O God, may all the peoples praise you...then the land will yield its harvest, and God, our God, will bless us. God will bless us, and all the ends of the Earth will fear him" (Psalms 67:1-7).

Christ directs us to seek first His Kingdom (Matthew 6:33). We can't get distracted from effective service in the Kingdom of Christ. The Father knows our needs. As we make the Kingdom a priority, He will make sure we meet our earthly needs. The pivotal reality of Christ's Kingdom is eternity! As the "Eternal King," Christ far exceeds any temporal authority placed in our lives!

It is all about the advancement of Christ's significant Kingdom—through us.

Friends, brothers and sisters, every one of us is a working member of the body of Christ. A joint here, a muscle there; we are designed to be a source of faith, love, money, grace, and glory—all meant to produce a stronger, healthier body of Christ! If one of us is blessed, the whole body is blessed! We all need a greater measure of God's glory in our lives! "Draw near to God, and he will draw near to you" (James 4:8). We have got to be about God's business!

Yes, Jesus Christ died for us, but He died to obtain something for us: entrance into the Kingdom of His Father. The Father's Kingdom has everything we could ever need or want; it is a Kingdom of inexhaustible supply! It's all about the Good News of the Kingdom of Heaven, not the Good News of Heaven! The two are not the same.

Jesus never preached Heaven! His disciples never preached Heaven! The Kingdom of Heaven is the rule of God *here on Earth*. The Kingdom of God is not a religion, but a relationship. It's about citizenship! It is the blood of Christ that makes this Kingdom effective! It is the blood of Christ that restores us to righteousness and holiness. The blood of Jesus is critical. We have to confess Jesus Christ as our Savior and Lord, and allow His blood to cover and cleanse us.

As children of God, we're part of the royal family of the Kingdom of Heaven. It is the job of the Holy Spirit to train and prepare us to become members of the royal family. We must be re-trained in the behavior and mindset of the Kingdom. We are a "chosen people," a "royal priesthood," and a "holy nation." We're being trained to represent the government of God on this Earth. We're ambassadors of the Kingdom of God.

Christ came to remove ignorance about His Kingdom, and to teach us our "heritage" and about our "kinship" as children of "Our Father." Jesus is the light of this world; and light means knowledge.

Daniel 7:18 says that "the saints of the Most High will receive the Kingdom and will possess it forever—yes, forever and ever." Every believer is a saint. If you are a saint, guess what? You are an heir to the Kingdom of God! The gospel of grace and the gospel of the Kingdom should never be separated!

Revelation unveils to us what the Lord has already done; not what He is going to do! Let's look at the Epistle of Paul to the Colossians, 1:13-14: "Who has delivered us from the power of darkness, and has translated us into His Kingdom of His dear Son, In whom we have redemption through His blood, even the forgiveness of sins."

Let us all stand up for the "majesty" of our King, Jesus Christ, as never before. Let us testify to His government more than ever. "To whom also He showed Himself alive after His passion by many infallible proofs, being seen of them forty days, and speaking of the things pertaining to the Kingdom of God" (Acts 1:3).

Christ alone is King! We have to advance the significance of God, advance the significance of Jesus Christ, advance His significant cause. And we have to accept His secured significance as sufficient. To God alone be the glory!

Obeying God's will is the greatest demand of the Bible. "Many are the plans in a man's heart, but it is the Lord's purpose that prevails" (Proverbs 19:21). Furthermore, "And I confer on you a Kingdom, just as my Father conferred one on me" (Luke 22:29).

Jesus came into this world to advance the significance of God's government. And He began His earthly mission, preaching and teaching "Repent, for the Kingdom of Heaven is near."

To God alone be all the glory.

May it be said of all of us that our lives are worthy, because to God alone be all the glory!

CHAPTER 11

The World Knew Him Not!

The gospel of Christ was the gospel Christ came to bring us. Jesus was a messenger sent from God with a message. That message was the Kingdom of God. This was the gospel of Christ. Jesus Christ is 100% King. We are not striving after originality! And I am not here to criticize; we just say that He is 100% King of the Kingdom of God!

Let's go to Mark 1:1-2: "The beginning of the gospel of Jesus Christ, the Son of God... Behold, I send my messenger before your face." John the Baptist prepares the way, as we see here in Mark 1:14-15: "Now after John was put in prison, Jesus came to Galilee, preaching the gospel of the Kingdom of God, and saying The Kingdom is fulfilled, and the Kingdom of God is at hand. Repent and believe in the gospel."

Well, let's talk about what is being said. Believe in the gospel. So you ask, "Pastor, is it necessary to believe *that* gospel to be saved?" So I ask you, "How can you believe it...unless you know what it is?" Many folks will sit in church listening to a gospel *about* Christ, but not the gospel *of* Christ! That's why I'm here presenting Jesus Christ to you as a sovereign, all-powerful, governing King who is to be OBEYED!

God of Heaven has set up a Kingdom that shall never be destroyed. This is the Kingdom of God! This is the gospel that is being suppressed and replaced by man's gospel of Christ! To have "distracted cares" is to distrust God for the future. God knows what is best for our good. In Luke 10:9, the "B" part of the verse is, "say to them, the Kingdom of God has come near to you."

Let's look at Luke 9:1. "Then He called His twelve disciples together and gave them power and authority over all demons, and to cure diseases." Acts 1:3 says, "...speaking of things pertaining to the Kingdom of God." Now let us look at Galatians 1:8-9 where God almighty, through Paul, pronounced a double curse on any man or angel that would dare preach any other gospel. Galatians 1:10 says, "For do I now persuade men, or God? Or do I seek to please men? For if I still pleased men, I would not be a bondservant of Christ."

The good news of the Kingdom of God is something that we at Gratitude Life have taken our time to help you understand and believe. The purpose of our church is to prepare "called-out ones" to go teach and to rule in the Kingdom of God. I'm here to tell you today that a counterfeit gospel is being passed around. There is some serious misrepresentation and deliberate confusion being presented to the world today as the Gospel! The bottom-line is that God is supreme—the 100% Ruler over all nations, governments, and kings with a little "k." Our God rules the universe! The FACT is, God rules; and that is absolutely, positively, beyond any doubt the truth of the Kingdom of God. This is the one and only true gospel of Jesus Christ.

I'm not here with a dry, dull, dead sermon; I'm here to proclaim a living, awesome, tremendous, vital, life-changing King—100% King and the Kingdom of God! The Kingdom of God is a real kingdom; it is a government. I get excited when I read in Luke 1:33, "And of His Kingdom there will be no end." He is the nobleman of the parable, who went to the throne of God—"the far country"—to be crowned as King of Kings over all nations, and then to return to Earth.

Look at Luke 19:12-27, and Acts 3:21, which states: "Whom Heaven must receive until the times of restoration of all things, which God has spoken by the mouth of all His holy prophets since the world began."

Restitution is restoring something to a former state or condition—in this case, the restoring of God's government on Earth. This is the gospel of Jesus Christ, the glorified Christ, the Christ we give all the glory and honor to! Not man, not programs, not showmanship—no rabbits coming out of hats, no performance. Just 100% King, 100% Christ, coming in all splendor—the supernatural power God Almighty!

So I ask you today, "What are you preaching, Pastor? Why would you dare listen to any other gospel, Christian?"

What glory! I thank God for you; I thank God a new day has arrived. God has the solution. God, is first and foremost of all, our creator. God is a ruler. God is an educator. God is absolute authority. Praise, honor and all the glory be to God and to Jesus Christ, forever and forever. That's what Gratitude Life is all about. We own up to God as our

God. Not a man or woman, not things, not possessions, not titles, not self-esteem, not any kind of self-worth. We live to give God the throne of our heart!

Isaiah says it this way in Isaiah 26:13, "O Lord our God, other lords beside Thee have had dominion over us, but by Thee only will we make mention of Thy name." The psalmist said, "O God, Thou art my God, early will I seek Thee" (Psalms 63:11).

Thank you, O God, for your majesty! God, in you alone are to be found true wisdom, real blessedness, perfect goodness and unspotted righteousness! Yes, when we are born again, we are born into the Government and Kingdom of God. I know firsthand that the very idea that the only relationship we have with Heaven is the one we experience at death is simply contrary to the Word of God.

When Jesus came, he proclaimed, "the Kingdom of Heaven is at hand" (Matthew 4:17). Well, let's ask ourselves today: what was he referring to? It is my belief that "at hand" means that God's Kingdom is close enough to touch from right where we are! Mark's gospel (Mark 1:14-15) says the same thing: Jesus come to Galilee preaching the gospel of the Kingdom of God, and the Kingdom of God is at hand.

Repent and believe in the Good News!

All I am presenting to you is in the Holy Bible. The opening of my eyes to the truth brought me to the crossroads of my life! God's truth means being "called out" of the world. All this "other" preaching is wrong! Jesus Christ says "repent." The purpose of repentance and Christ's returning to earth in supreme power and glory is to set up the Kingdom of God, and to restore the Government of God.

The time of understanding has come!

Zephaniah 3:9 says, "For then I will restore to the peoples a pure language, that they all may call on the name of the Lord, to serve him with one accord." Pastors, evangelists, teachers, apostles—we have got to get back to the 100% King, Jesus Christ, and the governing Kingdom of God. We've got to get back to God's way; we've got to get away from the "seems right to me" gospel, the human government, and look to our Creator's government—not human misgovernment.

Carter G. Woodson once wrote, "Freedom is not a bequest, it is a conquest." Truly, freedom is both a bequest *and* a conquest. Christianity establishes the fact that everything that is exists in principle, in completeness. Principle is the way things are in the spiritual world; in other words, the way God thinks of them. The eternal quest of man is for principles, for when he masters the principle of anything, he possesses the thing itself. Freedom is a bequest, then, in that these life principles exist for man's benefit.

The conquest of these principles through our comprehension of them is the promised freedom of Christianity. The disclosure of the spiritual world revealed by Christianity brings the end of our quest. We may now indeed find the "journey's end at every step." Christianity invites us to enter this realm of light, love, peace, and perfection, not at some future time, but now. Christianity is more than an evolution, it is a revolution. It reveals a spiritual creation in the consciousness of the Creator: perfect, eternal, finished. This Creation, like the mind of the Creator, is without "variableness or shadow of turning." Time and space conceptions of finite sense are eliminated as we put off "mortality," the race beliefs of life, "and put on immortality," God's consciousness of His universe.

Man is the central figure of the Kingdom; he is the "Son and heir" to all that the Father possesses.

CHAPTER 12

Don't Be Afraid of Your Trial!

Say out loud with me: "My King Jesus Christ, my Savior loves me unconditionally, through all my sins, because I've returned to His love!" Let's not pretend; let's be real! Say, "I love Jesus, and He knows it."

Don't be afraid of your trial. Jesus knows the outcome; and He's telling you, as He told Peter, "Hold fast, friend. I'm praying for you. When all the dust clears, you will be restored. I'm going to use you to build my church. I have an eternal purpose behind your sifting. It's all for my glory."

Jesus promised His disciples: "I appoint unto you a kingdom, and you will sit on thrones, that you may eat and drink at My table in My Kingdom." Jesus said that he would reserve seats for them at his dining table. That was a very powerful pledge of security. Then Jesus suddenly addressed Peter with this strange warning: "Simon, behold, Satan has desired to have you, that he may sift you as wheat" (Luke 22:31).

Jesus came into this world as God's seed of wheat! And His springing up after sifting is significant, for he is bringing forth a new reign of righteousness.

At the time, Israel was an agricultural society, so everyone was familiar with the grain-sifting process. Sifting is a purifying process, separating the bad and the useless from the good and fruitful. In my opinion, the devil thought Peter's faith would fail in the shaking! In Luke 22:33, Peter asks, "What harm can a little sifting do to me?" Perhaps now you are facing a deep trial, an unexplainable shaking; you're being turned upside down, inside out, and maybe you think it's because of some evil in you. Yet the whole time, it's the devil sifting you like wheat—by God's permission!

Moreover, we have this assurance: the only people the Lord allows to be sifted are those he chooses to rebuild His fallen church! I never knew there could be something far more trying than spiritual warfare; but now I know it's the sifting process! Sifting is hand-to-hand combat with Satan himself.

Jesus said, "He that has no sword, let him sell his garment, and buy one" (Luke 22:36). Jesus Christ said, "I've protected you—but now you must pick up a spiritual sword and fight the good fight of faith." Jesus makes this oath to pray us through. He assured Peter, just like He is assuring you and me today, "I have prayed for you, that thy faith fail not" (Luke 22:32).

How quickly we forget God's great deliverance in our lives! How easily we take for granted the miracles He performed in our past. I share this message to help you find new strength for your present trial. Remember your deliverances! From Genesis to Revelation, God's Word literally screams at us to remember, remember, remember. It is for our own benefit that God tells us to remember.

Are you facing a crisis? Is there a menacing giant of a problem in your home, at work, at your business, in your family? That's why I have chosen to speak very plainly, to be very flat-footed, very straightforward with you.

Gratitude Life has one purpose for existence, and that is to share with you the majesty and glory of having Jesus Christ in your life! We have to remind each other of how great God is—of what He has done in the past to deliver all who trusted Him. Remember His wonderful work, and thank Him. Get a vision of His majesty and His glory and thank Him! Understand what God has put on the line for us.

Does God love us? He sent His only begotten son to suffer and then die for us! Doesn't He have a right to ask us to endure our trials?

When God talks about Zadok in 1 Samuel 2:35, He uses the word "forever." We are to be kings and priests forever. That is why even in the midst of siftings and trials we must remain…loyal! It is up to us to help Jesus Christ restore all things and teach all nations about God's spiritual family. We are the sons and daughters of God. We are kings and priests. Look at our potential! We need to submit to His every correction He sends into our lives, and be thankful for the trials and siftings! What a blessing it is to be corrected by our Father, no matter how difficult the trial!

Clearly, God allows His servants to go through deep waters, enduring crises they can't comprehend, so they'll be a testimony and comfort to others. It is the sifted brothers and sisters that help rebuild those parts of God's house that have fallen down!

Think about this: Peter's sifting had nothing to do with fleshly temptations like lust, greed, or covetousness. The attack was meant to undermine God's promises to this man. Satan wanted Peter to be convinced he was totally unworthy of Jesus' pledge to Him of Heaven. Imagine the lies the devil shouted at this broken man: "So you're Jesus' rock…yeah, right! So you're going to raise up a church? Look at you—you're a weakling, a crybaby, a person who denied the very one who called you and loved you. If you think for one moment you're going to sit at Jesus' table, you're nuts! You're not worthy of His promises. Your life is over!"

Yet—yet—thank you, Lord God Almighty—yet. Little did Peter know that he was being equipped with a vital message for the new church.

Paul learned from his trials. He learned to preach not himself, but Christ alone. By this point in his life, he'd stopped focusing on himself.

Gratitude: thank you, Jesus Christ, we devote ourselves completely to exalting Jesus our King! And I can tell you a place of gratitude is a wonderful place to be; where you're totally abased, yet full of revelation, light, and a vision of God's glory.

Paul says the sifting in our lives is for the safety of others: "For all things are for your sakes, that the abundant grace might through thanksgiving of many redound to the glory of God…and eternal weight of glory" (2 Corinthians 4:15-17).

Peter tells us we are not to be ignorant of Satan's devices. Jesus exposed one of the enemy's biggest devices when he said to John, "blessed is he who isn't 'offended' in me." By offended, he meant tripped up, trapped, tried, ensnared. Jesus was saying, "Don't entertain his lies!"

And let me ask you, what was Jesus saying to John? "Offended in me?" What was the devil after? What was the trial all about? Why do you think you're being tried? The devil wants you to speak three words: three words that would undo all prophecies, that would undo all the good that God has accomplished in John's life and in our lives!

What are the three words? "I Have Regrets." Regrets are unfulfilled expectations. "My hopes have not been met."

Well, impatience is a tool of the enemy! Impatience is the inability to wait or bear afflictions calmly. Impatient believers are offended when they see God working miracles all around them but not in their lives. They are offended when they believe God is slow to answer them. Yes, God's promises can try us at times, and that is when we need to add patience to our faith, during these times of trials and siftings! Otherwise, we'll end up offended at God!

Proverbs 18:19 says, "a brother offended is harder to be won than a strong city, and their contentions are like the bars to a castle." We spend out of faith in God completely when offended! But James shares with us the cure: "My brother, my sister, count it all joy when you fall into divers temptations, know this, that the trying of your faith works patience. Let patience have her perfect work!"

Bring your doubts to Jesus. Jesus loves you. Jesus knows what you need. Jesus is the Christ, Jesus is the King. Say with me: "I have no regrets; Christ has fulfilled all my expectations! God is mighty. God is more than able to meet our needs. God is pledged to hear our cries through our trials, and our sifting process!" I can tell you myself that He will hear, and He will answer! He is absolutely an expert in all areas of our human experience. He created everything, and he understands everything.

Prayer is not restricted to special people. Today God is saying to you, "Call to me and I will answer you, and show you great and mighty things, which you do not know!" He wants to lift us up today. Romans 16:20 says, "The God of peace will crush Satan under your feet shortly"!

This is your opportunity to go beyond ordinary prayer and into the supernatural realms of prayer to touch God and release the supernatural in your life. Here it is, July 26, 2011 as I write this, and I don't believe there has been a greater time for prayer in history, from the time God said "Let there be light" until today. The need for the people of God to truly learn how to pray has never before been bigger. I am convinced that normal little cute, memorized Church prayers are insufficient to provide this world with the Spiritual Breakthroughs that we must have now. Ordinary prayers are not working. There must be a supernatural manifestation of God's Spirit within the Body of Christ, moving us to a higher dimension of prayer.

God is raising up a Prayer Army that will pray on a new level, as if the salvation of the world depended on them. This is what we need today: a Prayer Burden for the World. Don't you want to see the world "shake" with the power of God?

CHAPTER **13**

Now Would Be a Good Time

Doubt is the sin that God hates the most!

Both the Old and New Testaments reflect that our doubting grieves God; it provokes Him, and causes the most pain. God has a heart of love. His purpose from the very beginning has been to reach a lost humankind. God chose us "before the foundation of the world" (Ephesians 1:4). God desired to shape a "first generation" that would trust him fully. He created us in His image and likeness.

There is only one God. He works His wonders through a believing people! The Lord will not work through a people who are full of doubt and unbelief. Hebrews 11:6: "Without faith it is impossible to please Him." Matthew 13:58 tells us that Jesus was Himself prevented from working wonders when the people didn't believe: "He did not many mighty works there because of their unbelief."

A few years ago, the Holy Spirit called me to start Gratitude Life Radio Ministry. God promised me that if I accepted the challenge, he would see to it that God-hungry people would tune in every Sunday morning—here in the Nashville area, and in time, around the world! We would never lack for money or have to beg for finances. God has been faithful! This ministry has no debt! But we need the regular monthly support of caring listeners of these messages. Special thanks to those who came through with very substantial support! You know who you are! We're much in prayer for all finances, yet we know that God will meet all our present needs. We have no other source of income, and this ministry is worth supporting; we pray diligently over every prayer request sent to us. Even if you are unable to give now, we'll gladly pray for you and your needs.

Beloved, the Lord did not save us simply so we could bask endlessly in His goodness, mercy and glory. He had an eternal purpose in choosing each one of us. He is searching for a believing, trusting people that He can shape as His greatest evangelistic tool! Our Lord does not use angels to witness His glory. He uses His people, and he desires to train us as a special, "peculiar" breed (1 Peter 2:9). That's why Gratitude Life is on the air. Yes, we have been rocked by hard times, broken by deep trial and various challenges, yet we continue to trust Him! That is what we are: "gospel messengers," people who are not fearful—not doubting and un-tested! And I know today, the world is listening and watching as His servants endure trials and testings while clinging to Christ!

But guess what? There is a place in Christ where there is no anxiety about the future. In this place there is no fear of sudden calamity, of affliction, of unemployment, no fear of a bad health report. There is no fear of the economy, the weather, etc. This place is one of total confidence in God's faithfulness! The writer of Hebrews calls it a place of perfect rest. Such perfect rest was offered to Israel. But the people's doubt and unbelief kept them out of God's rest. "They to whom it was first preached entered not in because of unbelief" (Hebrews 4:6). "There remains therefore a rest to the people of God" (Hebrews 4:9).

What is God telling us? That this offer of rest is for us even today! There still exists a place in you and me where doubt and fear no longer exists. This is a place of perfect rest; God is in total control of everything concerning you! Living in God's perfect rest is a way of life. He wants us to be maintained by His peace and His confidence in all our trials, knowing full well our High Priest is touched by the feelings of our infirmities. It's about learning to trust His promise to be faithful towards us in all things!

I can honestly tell you, I have no need for a title, or a big congregation. I have a few loyal friends and relatives who over the years have come to know that. I want to be a soldier who's fully prepared for the battlefield. I know that victory is won long before the battle begins! It's won in boot camp, in training and conditioning. I have lived enough to know I will always need Heaven's resources to help me endure! I am convinced of God's 100% absolute love for me and you today—unconditional love! I know that our Father gives grace when it's needed. God dispenses His grace through revelations in our trials, revelations that we could never in a million years understand in all our good times! I believe revelation comes to every praying, hurting servant in his or her time of need.

The Holy Spirit says "Jesus holds all keys to life and death." Sounds like to me that everyone's departure rests in His hand! Christ alone determines our eternal destiny! This message today is meant to bring peace to our hearts. Look at Jesus Christ: right now, standing before us, holding the keys to life and death, assuring us, "Don't be afraid – I hold the keys."

Something absolutely marvelous, fantastic, and exciting happens when we don't doubt, but simply trust God! God dispenses His grace through His people! Ephesians 4:7 says, "Unto every one of us is given grace according to the measure of the gift of Christ!"

So I say to you that we at Gratitude Life love you; we genuinely love you, we pray for you. We are standing with you. I say that today for a special reason, as when I recorded this, we were in the holiday season. Sometimes when I read the Book of Job, I get deeply troubled. I was angry at how terrible Job's so-called friends treated him in the midst of his grief. These men told Job (Job 8:6), "If you were pure and upright, surely now He would awake for you, and make the habitation of your righteousness prosperous." In Job 8:13, they said, "You've forgotten God, Job. You're a hypocrite." Later, in Verse 11:2-3, they told him: "You're getting less than what your sin deserves."

But guess what I like about Brother Job: he clung to his trust in God, he became a grace giver—and he lived another 140 years!

Doubt. Doubt. Doubt. The sin that God hates the most!

Our Lord moves every minute of the day supernaturally on our behalf, delivering us from the enemy. God is willing to work with us if we work with Him.

Say with me today: "My Savior Jesus Christ loves me unconditionally, through all my sins. Even though I've failed Him, He knows I still love Him with all my heart. This is the beginning of a wonderful new life." If you said that today, trust Him! Romans 10:13 tells us, "For whoever calls on the Lord shall be saved"! Doubt and unbelief is the worst sin of all. "God has not given us the spirit of fear; but of power, and of love, and a sound mind" (2 Timothy 1:7).

We serve a God for whom nothing is impossible. Romans 8:28 tells us, "And we know that all things work together for good to those who love God, to those who are called according to His purpose."

If you truly believe God loves you, and you lay all your cares on Him, you can walk in glorious freedom. Free dominion. Agreement is the law of Christianity, because it is unity and unity is love. God is life and all life is on the inside of this universal life. The thing which finite senses imperfectly perceive exists in perfection in divine Mind. In spiritual creation, there is nothing and no one to disagree with; agreement extends to the relationship between man and man. Only in affiliation can we accomplish our purposes with each other. "Again I say unto you, that if two of you shall agree on Earth as touching anything that they shall ask, it shall be done for them of my Father which is in Heaven" (Matthew 18:19).

Since life is One and that One pure Spirit, there can be nothing to disagree with; therefore we are told to "resist not evil" and to agree with even our adversary. The adversary can be nothing but a wrong belief, "the devil," therefore instantly agree with it; it is nothing, and there is nothing to oppose our full expression of life. Thus we take all power to harm us out of everything or any one. The only power the adversary has, we give it by our belief in it as power.

All power is God's; there can be no other power. In disagreement we repel; in agreement we receive and attract. The former holds us in bondage to evil beliefs, the latter enables us to live the life of truth and freedom. To live in spirit and in truth gives us the "New Tongues" of Christianity. Life, love, competency, power, truth—those are the life-bringing words of the New Era; sin, sorrow, materiality, death are the obsolete language of our former ignorance.

The great discovery of Jesus was, "The flesh profiteth nothing." The life of man and his body are in Spirit alone. "Satan hath bound him," Jesus said of the one who was under the material delusion, being rendered impotent by the limitations of his own erroneous beliefs. "It is the Spirit that quickeneth"—that is, changing our material belief of body to a spiritual conception of it.

Forgiveness of sin is the Biblical term for correcting our misconceptions of life to the Truth. We correct our material errors in direct ratio to our perception of God's finished Creation. This is another of Christianity's revolutionary ideas: that it is man, not God, that forgives sin. It is the false concept of life which has sinned, and man's perception of Reality enables him to correct the errors of sense, in both his own mentality and that of others. There is no forgiveness of sin, save as the sin is corrected and abandoned.

Man's responsibility is clearly defined in Christianity. "Whose soever sins ye remit, they are remitted unto them: and whose soever sins ye retain, they are retained" (John 20:23). Every advance of the human family is by the correction of the errors in the thought of the race. As we make our accounts tally by making them square with the principle of mathematics, and correct our unmusical discords by the fixed fundamental rules of music, we forgive sin, a violation of spiritual law by the application of the unerring accuracy of spiritual principles. This restores us to unity, peace, and truth; a false sense of life miscreates "all the ills that flesh is heir to." True vision enables us to live in God's eternal love and life.

To "heal the sick, cleanse the lepers, raise the dead, cast out devils," is the natural result of the forgiveness of sin. In fact there is nothing to cast out but sin (an evil belief), and wholeness results. The whole process which confronts the Christian worker is to hold consciously in vision the real, thus giving to one's self the supreme joy of knowing that "I have filled the unforgiving minute with sixty seconds' worth of distance run."

For joy—radiant, soul-filling joy—is the purpose of Christianity. "These things have I spoken unto you, that my joy might be in you, and that your joy might be full" (John 15:11). Life is an ecstasy and of unfailing interest while we remain with the vision. Nothing is hopeless, and our service to the race is incalculable in its light, for every one that *sees* aids in the freeing of the race from its delusion of power in the material misconceptions.

Every one of us is a distant thought in God consciousness, a channel through which an idea is to be expressed. Frederick Froebel, the apostle of individuality, says: "Every human being has but one thought peculiarly and predominantly his own, one fundamental thought, as it were, of his whole being, the keynote of his life's symphony, a thought which he simply seeks to express and render clear with the help of a thousand other thoughts, with the help of all he does."

Life is a symphony and each has his part in it, and not to yield ourselves without reservation to the Power is to fail "to do the will" which enables us to "know the doctrine." As we individually emerge from the isolation of the self to the unison of the Self, the stately and harmonious rhythm of the great solar systems each majestically "about the Father's business" will be apparent in our lives. Then in the universal birth of the Christ idea may the angelic anthem be heard, "Peace on Earth, good will to men."

God bless you.

CHAPTER 14

He Made Us Kings and Priests

"He made us kings and priests unto God and His Father; to Him be the glory and dominion for ever and ever" (Revelation 1:6).

He made us kings and priests. Everyone who calls himself or herself by God's name is to be a priest unto the Lord. Everyone who loves by the name of Jesus should be learning to hear God's voice. He wants you to hear His voice, hear His word in your own heart! "And I will raise me up a faithful priest who shall do according to that which is in mine heart and in my mind. And I will build him a sure house; and he shall work before mine anointed for ever" (1 Samuel 2:35).

This holy ministry is the Zadok priesthood! It is made up of faithful, holy ministers of God who walk and live according to His desire. Zadok's name means "one who is righteous, one who is 'proved' righteous." God made a promise in His Word that if His people would repent and return to Him with all their hearts, all their hearts, He would raise up for them "Zadok shepherds." "Turn, O backsliding children, says the Lord....and I will bring you to Zion; and I will give you pastors according to mine heart, which shall feed you with knowledge and understanding" (Jeremiah 3:14-15)

Ezekiel prophesied that a Zadok priesthood would be very much alive and well in the last days: "But...the sons of Zadok, that kept the charge of my sanctuary when the children of Israel went astray from me, they shall come near to me to minister unto me, and they shall stand before me to offer unto me the fat and the blood, said the Lord God: they shall enter into my sanctuary, and they shall come near to my table, to minister unto me, and they shall keep my charge" (Ezekiel 44:15-16) .

This Zadok priesthood will be fearless against sin—and will have the power to lead people into righteousness and holiness. They will make it clear what right and wrong are, until you gain the knowledge and wisdom to make right choices! They don't pray "Bless me, bless my programs, give me money, be my partner and let me continue to cater to my own needs." These are churches and ministries afraid to offend anyone, instead catering to people's weaknesses and cravings, feathering their own nests! This is a picture of a compromising priesthood—afraid the offerings will go down, and maybe you'll lose your income! It is time the body of Christ discerns the difference between holy and phony ministry! We need to know what a ministry after God's own heart looks like.

There is something new happening over here. It's a new move of God; it's your ticket to great success and unlimited prosperity. No reproof over here; we're active, we're busy, and we're growing a large congregation. My pastor wears $2,000 suits, drives big cars, lives in a palace, and we're chasing after the same things! Bling, bling, bling! Self exaltation and pride; "then Adonijah...exalted himself" (1 Kings 1:5) It was self-centeredness, it was pride; Please Realize "I" Desire Exaltation! Adonijah says, "I will set myself up as a king!" Adonijah surrounded himself with ungodly men! This was a group of self-serving, success-driven, ego-stroking rebels.

I share with my pastor friends to continually be on your faces, weeping before God. That is how your church will be blessed. Don't get caught up in a fleshly, ungodly work. You see, when God wants to do something that really counts for His eternal purposes, He calls on those who have been shut in with Him. Every so-called minister who is puffed up with pride, compromising himself, only concerned for the welfare of himself, will know three Judgments: he will lose all spiritual authority; he will be bypassed by the true anointing and blessing of God in the last days; and he will lose God's touch in the very prime of his life.

To be "lightly esteemed" by the Lord means a loss of God's favor and blessing! No impact against Satan's kingdom! You're esteemed by "others," but in God's eyes you're a lightweight—someone in whom He puts no trust! "When I use the time to pour out my spirit, you will be standing in ruins"!

Look around you, brothers and sisters: preachers are standing in churches that are spiritually dead, dry and ruined! The parking lots are full, the pews rocking to worldly entertainment. But God has said to them, "I will pass you by!" These people will be bypassed and left to play their church games. You are lightly esteemed; go about your ministry with no real spiritual authority, and all the increase of your house will die in the prime of life. At a point when you ought to be at your best, ready to be used the most, a spiritual death will take place.

Works of the flesh only look good, making everything sound like important church work; but God refuses to touch it! Zadok says, "I don't want any part of that kind of ministry. God has gone from it." Zadok was the first young priest to recognize God's anointing on David's life (1 Chronicles 12:1-8).

Thank God, thank God, thank *God* there are men and women like that in the pulpit today. They are committed to Jesus as King! They have walked away from all flesh, entertainment, and worldliness! And you know it when you hear them preach, because something registers in your soul. Can you hear His word in your own heart? Can you say, "I'm hearing something good right now?" Aren't you tired of flesh? Oh God, give us the spirit of the Zadok priesthood...now!

I thank God for such pastors, bishops, apostles, and mentors. Tragically, few ministers today have the anointing of God's spirit. They may be able to tell a good story or memorize scripture...but they have no fresh word from Heaven. The Spirit of the Lord is about to bring a great cleansing, with new mercies—"and my church will once again be a place of joy and true praises, where all bondages are broken. I'm going to establish a multitude of godly priests in cities everywhere, and they will serve me in truth, causing my sheep to lie down in rest. There will be intimate, personal concern for every sheep. Those godly priests will care for God's people individually!"

No evangelist, no revival, no new movement will accomplish this. It will happen only by covenant promise! Jesus Christ has established His church: and its name is not Baptist, Pentecostal, Charismatic, or any other name but simply—The Lord, our righteousness! God said this church shall be a name of joy, a praise, and an honor before all the nations of the Earth, which shall hear all the good that I do unto them, and they shall fear and tremble for all the goodness and for all the prosperity—that "I" procure unto it, that "I" will make for them!

God is going to do "something" so amazing, so clearly full of abundant peace and truth, that people will tremble with fear! All fear and trembling would come through a "revelation" of God's goodness. Can you say Gratitude? Can you say, thank you very much, good God Almighty? It would come from an expression of His unmerited blessing. We see a picture of this holy trembling in Mark 4, when a storm threatens the disciples' lives. Jesus rebuked the wind and sea, saying, "peace, be still." The wind ceased; there was a great calm. They feared and said one to the other, "What manner of man is this, that even the wind and sea obey Him?" They trembled at what? The goodness of God.

Undeserving as we are, Gratitude Life is before God, thanking Him for the spirit living and working in us—and thanking Him, thanking Him, thanking Him very much for preparing us as Christ's Bride. With all our problems, failures, and quirks, the Lord is working in us. He is causing us to do His will; He is making us holy, blameless; He is letting Gratitude Life shine a light to the whole wide world. And for that, the Gratitude Life will stand by humbled with a holy fear, with a "Thank you Jesus!" shout! A "Thank you Lord, hallelujah!" for making us kings and priests unto God. For everyone who has been washed in the blood of Jesus has been raised up as a priest unto the Lord. God wants you to know right now, in the midst of your storm , that He stands beside you! He is feeding your soul! He is putting down His strong roots in you!

Your Father is preparing you for a great harvest! He has made us kings and priests. He wants us to hear His voice—to hear His word in our own hearts. He is building us a sure house. He promised to walk before His anointed kings and priests forever. Zadok means one who is "proved righteous." We do not want to be lightly esteemed, folks; we want God's covenant promises. We want to be a part of "the Lord our Righteousness Church!"

Kings and priests! You have meaning in your present life not because of your faith, not because you obey rules, not because you live right, but because you know Jesus! You are vitally connected to a loving King! You and I are devoted to a person, the Lord Jesus Christ. It's all about living with the King 24 hours of each and every day. Know Jesus, believe Jesus, Jesus alone. Now, say this with me: "Dear Jesus, thank you for dying for me. I accept your free gift of salvation. I want a relationship with you. Thanks, Jesus!"

CHAPTER 15

The Life That Wins

The life God gives us at the time we receive and believe in His son Jesus Christ is the life that wins! It is a life that overcomes sin. It is a life that provides intimate communion with God. It is a life full of satisfaction and power. It is a life already in you, waiting to be explored. Let go of yourself, and let Christ "live" instead of you! This requires a child-like faith. Enjoying this life that wins is awesome.

Paul shares with us in Galatians 2:20, "I have been crucified with Christ; and it is no longer I that live, but Christ lives in me. And that life which I now live in the flesh I live in faith, which is in the son of God." Can *you* say "Christ lives in me"? Paul says he has already arrived at this place. He has already possessed this experience. He has already entered in! He says,

1. I have been crucified with Christ;

2. That life I now live in the flesh I live in faith;

3. The faith which is in the son of God.

"I have been crucified in Christ." Tragically true; although Christ lives in us, we ourselves live in us too! In order to have Christ as our life that wins, we must move out and completely let go. And when we move out, we obtain this victorious life!

The issue is not religion, denomination, what kind of car you drive, how big your house is, no; the issue is you moving out! Romans 7 unveils a hidden flaw in us, which is to say we do not approve of what God has done and we do not accept His verdict.

Why did God crucify us when he crucified His son? He was telling us we were absolutely useless: that we were beyond repair or improvement. This was God's appraisal of you and me! I, like Paul, had to learn to accept God's evaluation of us. Today, let us realize that the cross expresses God's despair of men and women! Let us stop claiming we are not so bad, that we only sin just a little. We make resolution after resolution, yet we always fail. We have resolved and made promises long enough!

"I have been crucified with Christ" means that God was disappointed with us. We too must reckon our goodness and our self-worth as helpless and hopeless, and let us confess with Paul that we could never please God. I am finished! I am finished. This is the essential condition for victory! We now have to believe, "that life which I now live in flesh I live in faith, the faith which is in the son of God."

Christ is our head. Do you believe that today? We are members of His body. Do you believe that today? Do you believe that Christ our head is feeling, caring for, and controlling us? Christ is the vine, and we are the branches (John 15:5). The fruit-producing power is in His life, which is our head, and we are His members; we are His branches. He is supplying to us His life that wins! We do not have to establish our own holiness. We must submit to God's holiness. Christ is our victory, for victory is Christ. We have to move out of the way, we have to yield. We have to believe – and Christ will live out His victory in us.

O God I thank you, I give you praise, I am filled with gratitude that I can believe your word—instead of my feelings!

Oscar, sanctify my people in truth—my Word is truth. The life that wins is far superior to "our" experience. The God-given life that wins is Jesus Christ. It is all about exchange, not change. He is the life that wins! We now fight "from" victory, not fight "to" victory! We must fight "from" victory; victory is totally dependent upon Christ.

The great goal before us is "be not fashioned according to this world, but be you transformed by the renewing of your mind, that you may prove what is the good and acceptable and perfect will of God" (Romans 12:2).

As an apostle of Jesus Christ, Paul was also a commissioner of Jesus, functioning with Christ. Paul was involved in the Divine Government as a department head. He did not seek to be served; he became a servant. He did not demand a salary; instead, he supported himself as a tentmaker. Paul possessed a keen sense of togetherness with

Jesus—the head and the body together! We need each other as members of the same body!

Brothers and sisters, the truth is powerful; genuine truth can be tested. There is a great deception that is born of human tradition that is causing major confusion in this mixed-up world. Please take time to think about where you're headed—and about whether Christ is in your head! Make no mistake about it, Jesus Christ our head, is our Savior. Jesus was Immanuel, God with us. Jesus is our daily intercessor; Jesus is our soon-coming King. We must come to know Christ as the life that wins!

Every day that God permits us to wake up, He has a good day planned for us. We need to learn to trust this truth! All of our so-called life problems are man-made. Trust in God! Quit sabotaging His plans and life will be simpler and better! Glory be to God!

CHAPTER 16

Self-Inflicted Nonsense & Heavenly Vision

I was not disobedient to the heavenly vision! Paul hinged all his behavior on this heavenly vision. Today, if you know what's good for you, you must stay with the Bible: Basic Instruction Before Leaving Earth! We recognize that God's word will not return void. The strongest, most helpful thing I can give you today is the word of God, line upon line, precept upon precept, as we teach and preach from the Bible.

The Book of Acts is the book of the continuing work of Jesus Christ in the person of the Holy Spirit. Luke, who wrote this book, was a very close associate of Paul. In Acts 26:2, Paul begins to speak: "I think myself happy, King Agrippa, because I shall answer for myself this day!" This gives special attention to the expression, "I was not disobedient to the heavenly vision." Everything begins with God; the clearer our vision of God, the clearer everything else in life will be. Everything rises and falls on leadership, and guess what? Leadership rises or falls on our vision of God!

Go to Isaiah 6: Isaiah saw the Lord on a throne, high and exalted! Remember, our vision of God determines everything else! Proverbs 29:18: "Where there is no vision, the people perish." Vision is a discerning matter, where discernment means to detect with the eyes, to recognize mentally. Vision is a defining matter. Definition: to clarify. Vision is a refining matter. Refinement: to free from impurities, reduce to a pure state.

How do you see Jesus Christ right this minute? Do you see Him as a baby in a manger? Do you see Him on a cross? Do you see Him bleeding and dying? Well, let me share with you how the Bible declares we should see Him, in Hebrews 8:1: "Now of the things which we have spoken this is the sum; we have such a high priest, who is set on the right hand of the throne of the majesty in the Heavens." This is what we are told in this chapter of the Bible:

1. He came to this Earth without ceasing to be God.

2. He was robed in flesh.

3. He owed no sin debt of his own.

4. He was buried in a borrowed tomb.

5. He arose from the grave alive.

Well, how great is your God? What vision do you have of Him? This is what Paul is speaking about in Acts 26, concerning his salvation when all his religious endeavors left him lost. It was all sin—S-I-N, Self Inflicting Nonsense! And guess what, your sin, your Self Inflicting Nonsense, will leave you the same way! I know, because it did me the same way. It will leave us lost without God and without hope.

Gratitude Life is all about pursuing the right vision of God! We do not hold ourselves out as some kind of authority on church and ministry; however, we're serious on the matter of personal accountability to God. God is not our buddy! God is not our butler or a tradition, either. God is not Mr. Money Bags! He is the creator God, who spoke the world into existence, the God before whom we shall bow and confess that He is Lord! We've got to see. We've got to get a vision for what he truly is! We must enter into His presence with gratitude, thanksgiving, praise on our lips, a shout in our hearts. Truly, it creates in us total 100% accountability to God!

They came to Paul in splendor, the bling-bling, their royal gowns, all the trappings of success, King Agrippa and company. Today I can say to you—I would rather have had what Paul had that day than everything they had or ever could have in this world! Paul said he had seen the Lord for who He is, and he said before them: "I was not disobedient unto the Heavenly Vision." Vision means revelations; this is how God reveals himself to us! Whose vision are you following? So what if your church has 20,000 members; so what you have a TV show; so what, so what, so what?

The truth is, it's all sin. Sin: Self Inflicted Nonsense! We should all have God's heart in *our* hearts! All of us should be striving to understand something about the heart of God, and what God wants to accomplish in this world.

This is the vision Gratitude Life serves up to you today. It is this vision that brings us, black and white, rich or poor, sick or well, together in our accountability to God. We, like you, have a call of God upon our lives! Our vision is about being a blessing world-wide, not about things! The Lord truly has a mission in this world. Our work is to do His work! We at Gratitude Life are called first and foremost to be with Him (Mark 3:14).

There should be such Christ-likeness among God's people that strangers who come into contact with us sense His presence. All things are working together for the good of those who love God! Our work, our ministry, must be divinely directed and vision-directed; we must be God-directed from revelation! It is this vision that demands action—the Heavenly Vision!

Where was Paul? Was he at a conference? Was he bragging about how blessed or how good he was? Look at Acts 26:19-20: "Whereupon, O King Agrippa, I was not disobedient unto the Heavenly Vision: but first showed unto them of Damascus, and at Jerusalem, and throughout all the coasts of Judaea, and then to the Gentiles, that they should repent..." And do what? "...turn to God and do works meet for repentance"!

This was the message God gave Paul in Mark 16:15: "Go you into all the world, and preach the gospel to every creature." When we see the Lord high, exalted and lifted up, it creates this type of accountability to God and to God alone! We must do what God has given us to do. We have become at this point witnesses, and we must witness what we have seen as eyewitnesses!

You can't be a credible eyewitness if you haven't seen anything!

We've got to get in on what God is doing. We've got to get this gospel out. God is our goal. The task is not the goal, *God* is our goal! That is what Gratitude Life is about: taking action—speaking to people about Christ!

Back to Acts 26:1: "So Paul stretched out his hand and answered for himself." Do like Paul today; stretch out your hand and answer for yourself, saying, "I think myself happy! I shall answer for myself!" Acts

26:6-7: "And now I stand and am judged for the Hope of the promise made of God, to our fathers. To this promise our twelve tribes, earnestly serving God night and day, hope to attain for this Hope's sake." Paul was not disobedient to this Heavenly Vision. Paul knew he was in the center of God's will in jail.

Once we see what God is doing, we will want to get in on the action. I love where God has placed Gratitude Life. We are determined to grow this ministry as His servants. We will not be disobedient to the Heavenly Vision!

CHAPTER 17

Each of Us!

Each of us is called; each of us is chosen by God to play a very specific role in bringing about His kingdom on Earth. As 2 Timothy 1:9 tells us: God has "called us with a holy calling, not according to our works, but according to His own purpose and grace."

When you hear the use of the word "anointed," what is your initial reaction? There's a lot of confusion about the use of this word today. We need to see what the scriptures say about anointing, both in the Old and the New Testaments. We need to understand how the anointing enables us in our callings!

In the days of Moses and the prophets, when the sacred anointing oil was applied to a person or thing, they were set apart for God's purposes. Look at Exodus 30:23-24, where God told Moses how to compound the sacred anointing oil when He was speaking to him at Mt. Sinai. Later, the anointing oil was used by the prophets to anoint kings like Saul and David (1 Samuel 10:1, 16:13). The anointing oil was poured over their heads.

Why was oil a symbol of consecration? Because it was an element His people could relate to. Even common oil was precious and used in a variety of ways as an important part of people's lives!

1. Oil was used to give light.

2. Oil was used for provision.

3. Oil was used for healing.

4. Oil was used for beautifying, perfuming, and protecting the skin.

5. Oil was used to prevent sympathy in times of fasting.

6. Oil was used as a system of joy.

7. Oil was used as an act of worship.

8. Oil was used as a tithe, an offering to the Lord.

In a spiritual sense, the Holy Spirit is both our sacred and our common oil today. He anoints each of us to serve God. He anoints each of us to bring light, provision, beauty and healing to our lives. In each of us he takes away our need for sympathy. Each of us he crowns with joy. Each of us he leads into worship, and sanctifies our offerings. Under the new covenant our anointing comes from the presence of the Holy Spirit in our hearts! Jesus said, "it is expedient for you—for each of us...that I go away" (John 16:7) . Only after Jesus returned to the Father could that portion of God come into you and me! God says in Deuteronomy 32:30 and in Joshua 23:10 that if one of you connects with Me and My will, a thousand evil spirits can be put to flight! The scripture tells us Jesus learned obedience from what he suffered (Hebrews 5:8). Jesus recognized God's hands at every stage of His life.

Patience is not given to each of us! Patience is grown, if each of us will just realize God is so great, God is so mighty. He knows what He's doing in each of us, His purchased possessions!

The trouble with too many of us is that we think God called us to be manufacturers, when He really called us to be distributors. When it comes to ministry, all of us are bankrupt, and only God is rich! At Gratitude Life, we have come to accept ourselves as distributors of God's riches, and *not* as manufacturers! And guess what? We experience joy; we experience freedom in our service to you! We do not take any credit. If I as a pastor can explain what's going on, with the growth, the finances, and the leadership of this ministry, guess what? God didn't do it!

All I can say is, "the Lord has done great things for us, and we are glad" (Psalms 126: 3). We are thankful and filled with gratitude! We are going to let God have all the glory! It is our ministry to keep our chin up and our knees down! God is glorified when people meet the Master and not the minister!

Isaiah 42:8: "I am the Lord, that is my name: and my glory I will give to another." To each of us, let me suggest a vital piece of evidence that our work is glorifying God, and that the enemy opposes what we are doing. Paul announced, "for a great and effective door has opened to me, and there are many adversaries" (1 Corinthians 16:9). Each of us Purchased Possessions must remember: Christian service means invading a battleground, not a playground! God does not make us holy so that we can enjoy it. He makes us holy so that He can use us to do the work He wants us to do.

Each of us, Purchased Possessions! You know, Jesus died for a world that did not want Him. Why did he do it? Because it was the Father's will, and Jesus delighted to do the Father's will (Psalms 40:8). Serving God means being a part of a daily miracle! Serving God is the greatest work in the world! Each of us must serve others in God's name. At Gratitude Life, we have come to know that Christ is our answer—to *all* of our questions! He is the risen and victorious King of Kings. "O Lord, our Lord, how excellent is thy name in all the Earth!" (Psalm 8:1, 9). It is as though the psalmist has completely forgotten the fall of Adam and Eve, for he does not even allude to this and other negative facts! He leaps in thought across the whole history of redemption and cries, "How excellent, how excellent is thy name in all the earth!" The psalmist is at pains to underline this fact. God's purpose stands unaltered, and this excellence is to be known where? In all the Earth!

The creation of man was to meet the need of God. We've got to get back to Genesis 1—dominion kingdom, dominion living. Each of us, each day, must do something to contribute to the Kingdom of God! We have to build up God's Kingdom! Each of us! We can't keep ourselves back and contribute anything significant to God. God's purposes require a person who must undergo divine processes before being entrusted with the presentation of God's divine product, the gospel, to God's people!

Each of us must become commissioned representatives of the Living God. We can't take limited knowledge and start running with it; God's provisions awaits each of us, purchased possessions to mature as spirit-taught messengers! We don't want to be prodigals, which is to be need-oriented and self-energized and end up ruined in a far country, instead of having…"run with the footmen" (Jeremiah 12:5).

Each of us purchased possessions—each of us—needs to be patient and become fit vessels for the Master's service! God is always reaching down to man. Man is always striving up to God, and the Bible is the Book of the Meeting. This book grows in value to us as we grow in the knowledge of spiritual things; it interprets our spiritual experiences, and enables us to see the goal of mankind, the Resurrection of the human race, above material limitation and darkness. It is the inspiration alike for individual needs, national needs, and international aspirations. It inspires the artist, the literateur, the musician, the merchant, and the housewife. It comforts the sorrowing, and heals the sick in mind and body. It reveals our relation to God, and inspires our association with our fellow man to reach a closer affiliation. It is therefore not only the Book of the Meeting of God and man; it is the Book of the Meeting of man and man, for we never meet our fellow man until we meet him in Spirit.

CHAPTER 18

The Believer Priest

God made no provision for priesthood in the beginning. As long as Adam and Eve were in the Garden, they did not need a priest. Adam and Eve had an intimate, personal relationship with God. They walked and talked together in a knowing relationship. The first couple had fellowship with the voice of the Lord. Genesis 3:8 says, "And they heard the sound of the Lord God walking in the garden in the cool of the day." There was an impartation of knowledge, impartation being a transfer, sharing, giving, mentoring. God was Adam's only teacher. As long as Adam remained in intimate contact with God, his knowledge was unlimited. All the vast resources of God's knowledge were available to him as needed! Adam was completely open and transparent with God.

But sin disconnects us from God. How painfully Adam and Eve learned this lesson! Flagrant disobedience cost them their home in the Garden of Eden. But more importantly, it cost them their intimate relationship with God. We do well to remember that God's desire in creating Adam and Eve was for personal fellowship with them.

So let us now dig a little deeper. God had to institute a sacrificial system after that flagrant disobedience, just to restore a small portion of this fellowship. Let's look at Jeremiah 33:3: "Call to me, and I will answer you, and show you great and mighty things, which you do not know." He wants men and women whose minds are open to hear the voice of God. You can see that God is anxious for this intimate fellowship with us.

Let us look at what Paul wrote in 1 Corinthians 1:9: "God, who has called you into fellowship with His son Jesus Christ our Lord, is faithful." Now, let me say thank you! God is awesome; God bids us to enjoy times of friendship with Jesus. Neither you nor me, nor "our works," deserve this level of fellowship. Let's look at what James 2:23 says: "Abraham believed God, and it was imputed unto him for righteousness, and he was called the Friend of God."

Now, let's look at the concept and the nature of just what mercy is. God is merciful by nature. However, mercy does not overlook sin; mercy makes provision to bring persons *out* of sin. We're talking about the Believer Priest. God had to slay innocent animals as a substitute, and He had to sprinkle blood over Adam and Eve. He made coats from the animal skins to cover them, and this was now how Adam and Eve had to have fellowship, through an innocent sacrifice. This called for someone to make the sacrifice, and this person was called a priest. The priesthood came into being to help restore fellowship between Adam and Eve and God.

Adam and Eve were gloriously re-connected to God. And guess what? As the body of Christ, we are now re-connected to God, because of the complete work of Jesus Christ! We have been saved to serve—can you see that today?

That is our job here at Gratitude Life. In a most wonderful way, we not only service God, we actually serve God to you! The Believer Priest is a channel that brings the reality and presence of God to others. As the Believer Priest, you must help others learn to give thanks to God for what they have received. Memories seem to get very short when blessings are flowing! But we have no right to ask God for more until we learn how to say, "Thank you, thank you, Lord God Almighty!"

The Old Testament order of approach to God was "enter into His gates with thanksgiving, and into His courts with praise; be thankful unto Him and bless His most holy name" (Psalms 100:4). Just like it is useless to start talking on the phone until the dialed party answers, so it is useless to petition God until we are in His presence. The gateway to His presence is gratitude, thanksgiving and praise.

Adam was the first spiritual leader in history. God created Eve to fill an unmet need in Adam's otherwise perfect world. Eve restored her relationship with God, and today the Church is the Bride of Christ. We can all learn from Adam's mistake. We have to pay close attention to what God tells us!

Now let us look at another level of priests that God instituted to bring persons back into spiritual relationship with Himself: the fatherhood. The family was the government back in the day! The father was the ultimate authority; he was the family's access to God. Jesus became our substitute. He was the sacrifice; He is our priest (John 1:29). John makes this declaration, "Behold! The Lamb of God who takes away the sin of the world." Revelation 13:8 refers to Him as "the Lamb slain from the foundation of the world." This never needs to be repeated! His ministry of intercession in Heaven is eternal in nature. Thank you—hallelujah!

So the appeal goes out to you: Jesus, the 100% King, still needs Believer Priests. Who will join Him in making intercession for others according to God's revealed will? We don't work our way in; we believe our way in. This righteousness from God comes through faith in Jesus Christ to all who believe. There is no difference to all who believe.

It is faith in God's provision and promise that brings Christ's robe of righteousness as a replacement for our defilement—our deviation—our flagrant disobedience. The purpose of the Believer Priest is to restore relationship between people and God. Psalm 149:4 says, "For the Lord takes pleasure in His people." We are the objects of God's joy. Can you say "Thank you, God," today? Can you give God a heartfelt thanks today? Give thanks to God. In everything, give thanks!

God put Adam under authority so that he might learn obedience. God had ordered man to obey and not to be self-willed. Before Adam and Eve ate the forbidden fruit, their right and wrong was in God's hands. In eating the fruit, they found a source of right and wrong in something other than God Himself. That is what the Believer Priest and the work of redemption is all about. It is to bring us back to the place where we will now find our right and wrong in God. His word of command is authority! He accomplishes everything in it.

Obedience is a fundamental principle; the problem we all face is living outside the authority of God. The Believer Priest is to work towards recovering the oneness of the body of Christ. The greatest of God's demands on man is not for him to bear the cross, to serve, make offerings, or deny himself; the greatest demand is for him to obey God! God wants us to know His voice. Since Adam and Eve, God has been speaking to man. "They heard the voice of the Lord God."

As I break down this message, let me share with you a few insights: if you are living in sin, you will never hear God's voice! God's voice is so mighty...let's look at John 18:37: "Everyone that is of the truth hears my voice." Revelation 3:20 says, "Behold, I stand at the door, and knock: if any man hear my voice, and open the door, I will in come to him, and will sup with him, and he with me."

It is to believers that Christ is speaking. Open the door! Open the door! You know, every one of us has a little place in our hearts that we never open up to the Lord! Well, this is a room Jesus wants to visit you in today—so open the door! Jesus wants your closeness; He wants to sit down with you today. He says he will sup with you! Dinner for two.

That is what John 3:16 is all about: "For God so loved the world that he gave his only begotten son, that whosoever believes in Him should not perish, but have everlasting life." If your heart is sensitive to this message, it is a good sign that God is dealing with you. God has never, ever failed us!

CHAPTER 19

The Most Awesome Power of All

Experience the most life-changing power of the universe, the most awesome power of all, that of Kingdom Authority!

"I will guide thee with mine eye," Psalm 32:8 promises. "I will instruct you, I will teach you, I will show you the way to go: I will guide thee with mine eye."

Many brothers and sisters will know that the Lord has spoken personally to their present need! Our Lord wants a tested, suffering people who will rise up in the midst of trouble and distress and proclaim, "I trust my Lord!" God promises that His goodness is laid up for those of us who trust in Him before the sons of men! (Psalm 31:19). God's power to answer prayer is far beyond our ability to ask. This Kingdom Authority is a life changing concept! Can you imagine? God—our Father—wants to give us good things!

King David had a very unique approach to communicating with God: "Make haste, O God, to deliver me; make haste to help me, O Lord. Let them be ashamed and confounded who seek my life. Let them be turned back and confused who desire my hurt...O Lord, do not delay" (Psalm 70:1-2, 5). David never hesitated to ask God to hurry up and help him! To ask in Jesus' name means to ask by His authority! We must come to the throne in humility, on the authority of our Savior.

David cried out to God; he wanted God's guidance, not just an answer! "But the right and godly answer when he prayed." David wanted to "submit to God's will." We always need God's guidance, blessings and care. We need to be patient! Today we want instant gratification; BUT God knows what is best for us! He gives us the power, strength, and grace!

Let's look to Luke 6:46: Jesus asks, "Why do you call me, 'Lord, Lord,' and do not do what I say?" The Bible is the Word of God. We must come to a place of gratitude and come to appreciate that God's ability is limitless! We must pray for the Kingdom to come and thank

God for the blessings we already enjoy! Jesus said, "Seek you first the Kingdom of God, and His righteousness" (Matthew 6:33).

God's throne is established in authority! The acts of God issue from His throne. God's authority represents God Himself. Brothers and sisters, sin against authority and sin against power is sin against God Himself! We have got to know, it is *imperative* to know, how to serve God and to know the authority of God. For thine is the Kingdom, and the power and the what?...and the *glory*, forever, Amen. All Kingdom, authority, and glory being to God and to God alone. The Kingdom is God's.

My question is, how can we establish God's authority on earth if we ourselves have not met authority? Before he knew authority, Paul tried to wipe out the church. Before we can work for God, we must be "overturned" by His authority! Self cannot be the starting point for doing things in the name of the Lord. This is the activity of flesh!

Our Lord pronounces these works that are being done as acts of the evildoer, instead of His laborers! He emphasizes that only that person who does the will of His Father shall enter the Kingdom of Heaven. We are not to find work to do; rather, we are to be sent to work by God! The will of God is the absolute thing. We have to be subject to God's authority. The Lord's death is the highest expression of obedience to authority! The foundation is to O-B-E-Y God's will.

You can get careless with electricity if you want. Touch the wrong wires, and you will experience what an electric shock feels like. Your eyes will open to a great revelation! To see the importance of authority requires a great revelation as well! Even Jesus learned obedience through suffering. Every suffering he bore ripened into a fruit of obedience. Never once was Christ disobedient to God. Never once did He resist God's authority. He established God's Kingdom within the realm of His own obedience.

Believers would be best called "obeyers." According to Acts 22:10, after Paul had been enlightened he asked, "What shall I do, Lord?" When he was moved by the Holy Spirit to see the authority of the gospel, he addressed Jesus as Lord!

God never called the church to be an institution. He has ordained her to be the body of Christ. The physical head and its body are inseparable; they are forever one. God's intention for us is that we render complete obedience. Never try to set up your own authority!

God has never used a proud soul! Sooner or later, your pride will be revealed through your words. God only uses the useless! We who are sincere about the Father's business must never forget to stand on the ground of a servant. Therefore:

1. Reject pride.

2. Learn to be humble.

3. Learn to be gentle.

4. Never speak for yourself.

Stop grasping at fleshly authority: "I know so and so." "I preach to 20,000 folks." I, I, I, I...stop being I-minded. Stop trying to grab God's authority with your carnal hands. And keep this in mind: any restriction or disability in the church invariably limits God. Our concern should be God's work and God's way! I ask you today, is God free to work through you? Stop using the Bible for your own ends! Let's let our spirits be subdued by God. The most outstanding feature of the Bible is that God's spirit is released "through" this book!

We know Him as a Savior, but we must also know Him as a King. There is but one gospel that is relevant to our time, the gospel of the Kingdom of Christ. Thy Kingdom come. Let's stop postponing the Kingdom's arrival!

I will guide thee with mine eyes! I will guide you with my eyes! The word of God is sure. You can't be saved without believing God's word. You need not be afraid of God's authority! The word of God is trustworthy, whether spoken by Moses, Jesus, David, John, or Paul. John tells us in his first epistle: "He that believes in the son of God has the witness in himself. He that believes not God has made him alike, because he believes not the record that God gave His son!"

The king is the ultimate source of authority in a kingdom; and through this authority, a kingdom is established. Well, we must understand that the message of the Bible is about a King, a Kingdom, and His royal offspring. Jesus Christ is our King. Jesus Christ is our authority figure! Jesus Christ is King by birthright. Jesus Christ was not voted into power! Jesus Christ can't be voted out of power!

A decree of a king is unchanging. The king embodies the government of his kingdom. A king personally owns everything in his domain. Matthew 22:2: "The Kingdom of Heaven is like a king who prepared a wedding banquet for his son." And 1 Timothy 1:17: "Now to the King eternal, immortal, invisible, the only God, be honor and glory for ever and ever, Amen!"

Psalm 47:2 tells us, "How awesome is the Lord Most High, the great King over all the Earth!" And remember, in Psalm 32:8, He tells us, "I will guide thee with mine eye." We who are believers, who sit under the authority of Jesus Christ as king, must navigate between the Kingdom of Darkness, and walk diligently in the Kingdom of Light.

Chapter 20

How Excellent is Thy Name in All the Earth

Genesis 1, Psalms, and Hebrew 2 are vaguely linked together.

"How excellent is thy name in all the Earth." How excellent, how excellent!

Psalm 8 sings of God's plan for man in spite of the fall; the singer does not deviate! He reaffirms the original plan of Genesis 1. The dominion plan has not changed.

In Verse 1: "Our Lord, our Lord how excellent is thy name in all the Earth, Who has set the glory above the heavens." And again in Verse 9: "O Lord, our Lord how excellent is thy name in all the Earth!"

Verses 4-8: "What is man, that thou art mindful of Him? and the Son of Man, that thou visitest Him? For Thou hast made Him a little lower than the angels, and hast crowned Him with glory and honor. Thou madest Him to have dominion over the works of Thy hands; Thou has put all things under His feet: all sheep, oxen, beasts of the field, fowl of the air, fish of the sea and whatsoever passeth through the paths of the seas.

Verses 2-4: "Out of the mouth of babes and sucklings hast thou ordained strength because of thine enemies, that thou mightest still the enemy and the avenger. When I consider thy heavens, the works of Thy fingers, the moon and the stars which Thou has ordained; what is man, that thou are mindful of Him?"

Now let's look at Genesis 1:

In the beginning God created the heaven and the earth.

And the Spirit of God moved upon the face of the waters

And God said

And God saw

And God called

And God said

And God made

And God called

And God said

And God called

And God said

Verse 14. And God said

And God made

And God set

Verse 20. And God said

Verse 21. And God created

Verse 22. And God blessed

Verse 24. And God said

Verse 25. And God made

Verse 26. And God said

Verse 27. So God created man

Verse 28. And God blessed

Verse 29. And God said

Verse 31. And God saw everything that He made, and behold, it was very good.

Hebrews 2:1 tells us this: "Therefore we ought to give the more earnest heed to the things which we have heard, lest as any time we should let them slip."

Hebrews 2:8-12 declares: "Thou has put all things in subjection under His feet. He put all in subjection under Him; He left nothing that is not put under Him. But now we see not yet all things put under Him.

"But we see Jesus made...for the suffering of death, crowned with glory and honor; that He by the grace of God should taste death for every man.

"...bringing many sons unto glory, to make the Captain of their salvation perfect through sufferings.

"For both He that sanctifies and they who are sanctified are all of one," and Christ is not ashamed to call them brothers and sisters!

"Saying, I will not declare thy name unto my brethren, in the midst of the church will I sing praise unto thee."

Verses 14-18: "...He destroys him who had the power of death, and deliver them who were subject to bondage. He took on the seed of Abraham. ...He became the merciful and faithful high priest in things pertaining to God, to make reconciliation for the sins of the people. He himself suffered being tempted; He is able to succor them that are tempted."

Matthew 12:28 tells us, "But if I cast out devils by the Spirit of God, then the Kingdom of God is come unto you." Jeremiah says, "There will be a day when everything that stumbles men will be removed" (Jeremiah 31:9) .

Matthew 12:29: ..."or else how can we enter into a strong man's house, and spoil his goods, except first bind the strong man? Then he will spoil his house. "

These are significant statements; these are the "fruits" of the cross!

Genesis 1:26: "Let us make man in our image, after our likeness: and let them have dominion." Genesis 3 forward represents man's history, not God's purpose for him. A worker may fall from the top of a building under construction, but that was never in the architect's plan! God's plan is concerned with our dominion.

Adam was sent to the garden to "guard" God's paradise, which implies the proximity of an enemy to be kept at bay! The first thing man failed to control was a creeping thing! "Upon thy belly shall thou go, and dust shall you eat" (Genesis 3:14). But what is dust? It is the substance of which Adam was made. God's foe has secured legal rights to the Adam-made man—the old creation. So God meets this situation in redemption by bringing in a new creation, His new man. Jesus Christ being raised from the dead.

The Genesis 1 purpose lost in Genesis 3 is not lost for good! Genesis 1 man is on the throne! He is our King! "Thou crowned Him with glory and honor—how excellent is thy name in all the Earth."

Chapter 21

Stop Dancing With the Bear

Only the Father knows! Only the Father knows! The Book of Revelation came from a source higher than Jesus Christ. It came from the supreme Authority in the universe: God the Father! There is no other book that is introduced in the same manner as the Book of Revelation. It is the world that wants you to view the Book of Revelation like a horror movie.

"Apocalypse" means "an uncovering"—a disclosure to enlighten, or give light! This message will bring "light" to you. God the Father reveals this light only to "babes"—saints with child-like, teachable attitudes! Revelation 1:1-3 describes it this way: "The revelation of Jesus Christ, which God gave Him to show His servants things which must shortly take place; and He sent and signified it by His angel to His servant John who bore witness to the word of God, and to the testimony of Jesus Christ, to all things that he saw. Blessed is he who reads and those who hear the words of this prophecy, and keep those things which are written in it; for the time is near."

Matthew 24:33, 36: "So likewise you, when you see all these things, know that it is near, even at the doors... But of that day and hour no one knows, not even the angels of Heaven, but my Father only!" Only the Father knows; *only* the Father knows!

This is Christ talking. He is teaching us to understand that the Father is His superior! The Father has greater understanding, and that includes His knowledge of prophecy. Only the Father, *only* the Father, has the depth of understanding and foresight. In John 14:28, Christ says, "My Father is greater than I. I come to do the will of the Father." He came to do the will of His Father, not His own. He was 100% submissive to His Father.

In Malachi 1:6, God says, "A son honors his father and a servant his master. If then I am the Father, where is my honor? And if I am a master, where is my reverence? Says the Lord of Hosts to you, priests, who despise my name. Yet you say, in what way have we despised your name?" So now let's get over into the slow-down lane; let me share with you where the big bad bear is. It's "the world." And most of God's own people refuse to accept "our Father" as the head of His family! If you don't believe this, look around you today at church; you will not see God's family worshipping together. You will find black, white, Hispanic; you will find tribes of people, tribes that would give you the appearance that we are serving the gospel as one family under God our Father.

This is a satanic deception that destroys the very family of God! It destroys the gospel, which is the good news of the coming Kingdom, or family of God! Can we understand what Satan is doing? That is what Malachi is speaking about: a church that fails to honor their Father, a church rejecting God's family government!

The first verse of Revelation demonstrates God's royal family government. The Father is the head. Christ is the husband of the wife, or God's church. Those called after Christ returns are likened to the children. All together, it is God's family! There is a mountain of deceit revolving around Verse 1, so please don't speed-read Verse 1.

The greatest truth in all the Bible from my vantage point is this: it's all about God's royal family. Not about your family, not about a man on the corner who dresses well, speaks well, is someone who is charismatic. No, it's about God's royal family. According to Genesis 1:26, Man was made in the likeness of God, not animals. Animals were made after animal-kind. We were made in the likeness of God. We are God's family. We must serve the God family. Stop being religious; this is not a religious sermon. We must stop being deceived; it *must* be about the Father. God only reveals precious truth to His servants, His children, His babes!

The Book of Revelation depicts a world crisis, and how you can escape it! John was put in prison for teaching God's word and this testimony! So I ask you today, church leader, pastor, evangelist, worship leader—what is there about the testimony of Jesus Christ that could get you imprisoned or killed? What are you preaching? Prosperity, abundance—name it, claim it!

Revelation 1:9 says, "I, John, both your brother and companion in the tribulation and Kingdom and patience of Jesus Christ." Tribulation,

Kingdom, patience of Jesus. Christ was on the Island of Patmos for what? That is the question for the day: for what? Stop dancing with the bear, and answer this question: for what?

It was the word of God; it was for the testimony of Jesus Christ that John was put in prison! So today I ask, who is the head of your church? Church is about the testimony of Jesus Christ, not tradition, not programs, not tips on how to be prosperous, or how to draw big crowds! If you don't understand Revelation 1, you don't understand Christ! Without this understanding, we can't do God's work.

In Revelation 19:7, Christ's wife is making herself ready! Apostle John was in charge of God's church when he wrote the Book of Revelation. He said, "blessed is he that reads and those who hear the words of this prophecy." Notice what John is saying: he that reads, they that hear. He that reads: God uses "one-man" leadership. He reveals to only one man; then they who follow keep the truth that God reveals. This is God's way of government! It is 100% about the testimony of Jesus Christ.

Let's bring this in for a smooth landing by going over to Revelation 12:17: "And the dragon was enraged with the woman, and he went to make war with the rest of her offspring ..." Who what? "...keep the Commandments of God, and have the testimony of Jesus Christ." The offspring is "the remnant of her seed." Who was the remnant of her seed? Children of Jesus Christ—sons and daughters of God.

We at Gratitude Life are a small remnant of that woman's seed—Jesus Christ of Nazareth, with or without your support. We are determined to come to you in one way only, and that is through the truths of the word of God—the Bible! We are determined to keep God's lamp of truth burning brightly.

So I say to anyone that wants to understand the Bible and world events that will come, must come, to God's faithful remnant! There will be no understanding, no place else, from no one else on this planet. God works through His very elect, and no one else. Grace be unto you; gratitude be unto you.

CHAPTER 22

You Are Precious

You are precious to Him! Can you say with me, "My God delights in me"? Praise flows to you!

Let us read Psalm 18:16-19: "He sent from above, He took me, He drew me out of many waters. He delivered me from my strong enemy, and from them which hated me; for they were too strong for me... The Lord was my support. He brought me into a larger place; He delivered me because He was delighted in me."

David was looking back after a great deliverance. Let's go back up to Verse 3, Psalm 18: "I will call upon the Lord, who is worthy to be praised, so shall I be saved from mine enemies." This indeed was a time of terrible testing; the Holy Spirit gave David a revelation that is the key to all deliverance! My God delights in me! This is the key to *our* victory as well: God delights in us. We are precious to Him.

The Song of Solomon 7:6 states: "How fair and how pleasing art thou, O love, for delights!" In this context, "fair" means precious; "pleasing" indicates pleasure. This is how Jesus looks at His bride: "How beautiful, sweet and delightful you are, you are precious to me, O love!"

Gratitude Life has as its foundational goals a sincere desire to bring you truth so you will be able to understand what is ahead in this wicked time! There is a rest that God has promised us for every battle that rages in our souls; Isaiah says it this way in Isaiah 43:1-2, "Oh Israel, fear not, for I have redeemed thee. I have called thee by thy name: thou art mine. When you pass through water I will be with you; the rivers will not overflow you; when you walk through fire you will not be burned; neither shall the flame kindle upon you."

God wants me to tell you that you belong to Him! This trial or circumstance that you face is not going to destroy you. The true revelation is this. Look at Isaiah 43:4-5: "Since thou was precious in my sight, thou hast been honorable, and I have loved you...fear not, for I am with you!" God knows each one of us by name, and you are a delight in

His heart. God spoke a word to Israel, and He is speaking it to you on today: "You shall be a special treasure unto me above all people, for all the Earth is mine" (Exodus 19:5). We are God's special treasure. We are God's special and precious treasure.

That should make you grateful. That should bring back your hope. It does not matter: inmate, prostitute, dope dealer, it does not matter. You are precious to God. I want you to get a revelation of your preciousness in God's eyes! I'm not sure preciousness is a word, but it *is* a reality—and it is a key to a victorious spirit.

Jacob says in Numbers 14:8, "If the Lord delight in us, then He will bring us into this land, and give it to us." Don't focus on your condition, your problems, your weaknesses and inabilities; don't give in to your fears. God delights in you; He will lead you forward, for we are precious to Him! In recent days, the Holy Spirit has been leading me to pray for a greater understanding of God's love to me, and for the precious people who read this book that they may truly appreciate how much God loves them!

Listen to Brother Paul in Ephesians 5:2: "Walk in love, as Christ also hath loved us." We each have to walk as one who is greatly loved by God! As I prayed, I didn't know what to expect. Would it be a revelation? Would it be a feeling? Would it be a touch of His hand? No, God said, in a simple little word in John 3:16: "God so loved the world that he gave his only begotten son." He is a giving God. He invested His son Jesus; He gave Him to us. Christ is God's gift to us. He is all we need in order to be overcomers of every trial, test, and challenge we face today!

What sets us free, completely free, is seeing that the Kingdom is God's. Everything is God's, and so is the authority and the glory! No one, absolutely no one, can steal God's glory! When the Lord came to Earth, He came empty-handed! Every suffering that our Lord went through bore fruits of obedience. Jesus Christ came to this earth to establish God's Kingdom. The Lord Jesus Christ is the Kingdom of God. In Luke 17:21, Jesus says, "For behold, the Kingdom of God is in the midst of you." Without Jesus, there is no church; without the church, there is no expansion of the Kingdom of God!

God wants to see the Kingdom proceeding forth from the church. The church is the highway to the Kingdom. God's life, God's way, God's will, and God's commands must be executed in the church; that's when the Kingdom will come. When the church submits, the nations will submit! We're delaying God, we spiritual leaders. We must come to the end of "ourselves." We must acknowledge that we can do nothing, are nothing, and have nothing. We must realize that we are here *not* to be like the world, but to show the world what the Heavenly Kingdom is like! We must reflect the character of God's Kingdom. Authority is of God, and not us! May the Lord make us gracious, thankful people. Let us as servants seek God's grace. Let us be gracious to others. Let us be filled with gratitude as we share God's love with others!

As I bring this chapter to a close, let me say that you are precious. Brother, sister, pastor, evangelist, spiritual leader, you are precious to God; and today, please say with me: "My God delights in me!"

I have seen more about pride and self-exaltation and ego than I ever wanted to know! So today my prayer is: Lord, pride has also had residence in me. I denounce all forms of pride as you reveal them to me one-by-one. I believe that by identifying with your finished work at Calvary, I have been cleansed from the guilt of pride.

Now dear God, help me to learn to put on humility. Give me the servant spirit Jesus ministered in. Hold me to esteem others better than I esteem myself. I don't ever want to forget that I must be humble, or I'll stumble. Thank you, Amen.

CHAPTER 23

What a Privilege It Is

to Know How Awesome Our God Is!

We have to be about the business of the ministry of the King! The Words, the Works, the Ways. It's all about the King's goodness, grace and mercy.

The Words of Jesus are our richest treasure. They are our sacred trust. These Words are the best weapons of our spiritual warfare. The King's voice was strong enough for thousands to hear, yet gentle enough to have an infant hear His tender heart. He spoke as one having divine authority. He knew how to mingle meekness with majesty!

The Works: He came to lift the human family up! He selected, and instructed, and commissioned 12 Apostles to preach His gospel. Jesus saw the unpolished diamond in each of them!

The Ways: He taught the power of denouncing sin and the promise of pardon. He pointed out a light to console the obedient, and a flame to consume the disobedient. Truth was the instrument he made use of to transform, purify and elevate the human family!

The greatest threat to the future of this world is the world of religion. We have got to get back to the intention of our creator. Matthew 25:34: "The king will say to those on His right, Come, you who are blessed by my Father, take your inheritance, the Kingdom prepared for you since the creation of the world." God wants to share his Kingdom with his offspring, which he calls mankind—with His nature and character.

In the beginning, God! God has a right to the first place. Seek you first God, and everything else shall be added unto you.

Imagine wearing a pair of eyeglasses that enables us to see things differently; to see things from God's point of view. Now more than ever we need a way of life that brings us clarity in the chaos; peace in the problem; boldness in the bad times. We need God's point of view; we need God's perspective.

What a privilege it is to know how awesome our God is. What a privilege it is to dwell in the secret place of the most high. There is only one permanent supply, and that supply is God. The Kingdom of God is a Kingdom of immortality, eternity, life, and love!

Under Moses, there was the law. Under Jesus Christ, there is grace. The Kingdom of God is a Kingdom of grace. Human beings cannot receive God's grace! We have to permit the spirit of God to dwell in us. Romans 8:8-14 tells us that we have to be led by the spirit of God, to be a son of God!

We are talking about the life that wins. The spirit of God does not dwell in a person filled with envy, jealousy, malice, hate, or revenge. Remember Isaiah 26:3: "Thou will keep him in perfect peace, whose mind is stayed on thee!"

CHAPTER 24

Citizen of Heaven, Ambassador of God

When you are so convinced of the trustworthiness of Jesus Christ that you are willing to place your confidence in His trustworthiness, *then* you are ready to become a Christian. We are convinced of the total sufficiency of Jesus Christ. He is the only redeemer, and the Good News is complete in Him.

The Bible is the book God wants us to have. John 14:26 says, "The Holy Spirit, whom the Father will send in my name, He will teach you all things, and bring to you remembrance of all that I have said to you." In other words, Jesus Christ alone shall have binding authority over our lives. Jesus says, "I will never leave you, nor forsake you. Therefore, fear not, little flock, for it is your Father's good pleasure to give you the Kingdom."

We will get our greatest freedom from bondage to the "false" when we place our confidence in the Bible. The Bible is the word of God. Jesus Christ is our center; it is His truth that has been proven "substantial." The Bible invites us to enter and enjoy Kingdom living. From Moses to John, the Bible points us to the Lord Jesus Christ. The 24 hour Kingdom citizen, the 24 hour Christian, has an unshakable alliance with the truth…because of Jesus Christ. Our gospel is the good news of truth. The good news of love. We can rely on the trustworthiness of Jesus Christ.

It is a privilege to share with you and build a credible case for placing your faith in Christ. That is the ministry of the Gratitude Life. The Holy Spirit will complete and confirm the validity of our messages. The Holy Spirit is needed to bring man into spiritual touch with God!

Each of us has been given the gift of time: 24 hours a day. We have dominion over these 24 hours. Each of us are stewards of these 24 hours. The 24 hours we have each day should be treated as a gift.

Jesus is our companion. He is the source of our life. He is our friend; He knows us better then we know ourselves. And it is a great call to walk with Jesus and obey His will for our lives. Thank God today for His forgiveness and help.

The most important of time is Now! "Now is the judgment of this world; now shall the prince of this world be cast out. And I, if I be lifted up from the earth, will draw all men unto myself" (John 12:31-32). We have to begin now to take steps to position ourselves for victory instead of defeat. There are Christians who are not spiritually prepared to face the coming worldwide financial crisis, the Economic Armageddon! They have not become 24 hour citizens of God's Kingdom. They have not developed a covenant relationship with God. They do not trust Him to meet their daily needs.

We have to have total trust, total dependence upon Him...now. God works with a small remnant. God uses "one of a city, and two of a family," to do His end-time work. The 24-hour Kingdom citizens are God's most noble end-time warriors. We're a small remnant crying out in a wilderness of religious confusion.

"And I will give you pastors according to mine heart, which shall feed with knowledge and understanding " (Jeremiah 3:15). This 24-hour citizen of the Kingdom of God, the 24/7/365 citizen of Heaven, this 24-hour ambassador of God's divine government—it is happening right now! These 24-hour brothers and sisters in Christ are members of God's royal family. They're God's representatives—God's ambassadors.

Let me say this as a breakdown, the truths that are being shared: 1. The world refuses to submit to God's government; 2. The world rejects God's rule; and 3. Only God's government works. God the Father and Jesus Christ the Son have never had a serious government problem! They have been living in joyful unity for all eternity.

The work here at Gratitude Life is filled with hope. Many of God's family members are about to be born. It is a breathtaking honor to be family members in the body of Christ. Thank God for God's government! Thank God for God's Kingdom! Are you ready to make this the dominant theme of your life? God's church is a fortress that He will protect. We have nothing to fear if we obey God.

Citizen of Heaven, Ambassador of God 95

But—if we fail to obey God, then we are entering into a time when fear will be, by far, the most dominant theme of our lives! Having God's name in title, having God's name on the church sign, is not enough. God must be there too! Jesus had one message, and that was the Kingdom principle! God's government. He never preached prosperity, deliverance, or faith healing; he preached the born-again time! He said, "Repent, the Kingdom of Heaven has arrived." He did not come with news about religion, but about a Kingdom.

The greatest gift to all humanity is knowing Jesus Christ as King. God is creator. He is creating His family. God is present in a special way, in a powerful way. Pastors, evangelists, apostles, church leaders—we must trust God. We have to get back to where God wants us to be, spiritually. All the theater, performance, programs, all the attentions being placed on the messenger and not the message, is a disaster waiting to happen! We have got to get back to God's government. That is where new truth is being believed. This is where God is fulfilling His special covenant with ministries today (Jeremiah 33:21).

There is a great work to be done. A courageous and vigorous message must be delivered. God is the potter, and we must keep the big picture—that He is continuing to shape and mold us. God's goal is to always bring people to repentance. This has been and will always be a very unpopular message.

Are we preparing people to enter into the God family forever? We have to repent of our evil...bottom-line. We have to speak what God commands! No excuses! We must build on the sure foundation of God's government. "We are bound to thank God always for you, brethren, as it is meet, because that your faith groweth exceedingly, and the charity of every one of you all toward each other aboundeth" (2 Thessalonians 1:3). What a great compliment Paul paid the Thessalonian Christians! Here's the full essence of what he was saying: "It's incredible to see how much you've grown, both in your faith in Christ and in your love for one another. Everywhere I go, I brag to others about your spiritual growth. How I thank God for you!"

In this short passage, Paul gives us an amazing picture of a body of believers who were growing in unity and love. The Greek phrase Paul uses for "groweth exceedingly" means "growth over, above and beyond that of others." Both individually and corporately, the Thessalonians' faith and love outshone that of all other churches.

Obviously, these Thessalonian Christians weren't just trying to hang onto their faith till Jesus returned. They were learning, moving, growing—and their lives offered evidence to that fact. According to Paul, they were the talk of every church in Asia.

Apparently, the preaching these people heard was provoking them into an ever deeper walk with Christ. It was melting their fleshly ambitions and convicting them of un-Christlike habits. And the Holy Ghost in them was tearing down all ethnic barriers and color lines. They were discovering how to embrace any person, whether rich or poor, educated or uneducated. And they offered great care to each other, preferring one another in love. Moreover, the Thessalonian believers weren't easily drawn into error. They didn't allow false teachers to come into their midst and lead people away with fancy, new religious fads. They highly honored and revered God's word.

At the time, these Christians were under intense persecution. But that didn't stop other believers from visiting their extraordinary church. People descended on them in droves. Yet these visitors didn't come to be dazzled by signs and wonders, or to be awed by powerful preaching. No, they came to witness the great miracle of a church moving together as one body in the love of Christ. They wanted to see firsthand how a strong, steadfast gathering of believers was growing in the grace and knowledge of God.

Now, if Paul can compliment the church at Thessalonia, I believe I'm allowed to compliment our own congregation. I see and hear things among our body of believers that make me truly believe we're growing in the Lord "exceedingly."

If you're being watered and fed by God's word, you should have continual spiritual growth in your life. It should be happening automatically.

The anointed preaching of the pure word of God always produces growth. And the apostle Peter says that all who desire the pure milk of the word will grow. Paul describes our spiritual growth as a work of the

Holy Ghost. He says the Spirit is ever at work, changing us from glory to glory. He's constantly renewing our minds, shaming our flesh, and bringing forth purity in our inner man. He works in our hearts to put off anger, bitterness, resentment, and evil of all kinds. And he produces in us kindness, tenderness and forgiveness toward one another. He's growing us up in Christ—teaching us that everything we say and do has to be worthy of our Lord!

Paul further urges us, "Let a man examine himself..." (1 Corinthians 11:28). "Examine yourselves...prove your own selves..." (2 Corinthians 13:5). The Greek word for "examine" here means "scrutinize, test yourself." The apostle is saying, "Test yourself—see if you're walking according to God's word." We're to constantly ask ourselves, "Am I changing? Am I becoming more loving and tenderhearted? Am I treating my family and friends with godly respect? Is my conversation becoming more righteous, or am I still participating in dirty jokes? Am I still complaining, or am I speaking edifying words of faith?"

I take this matter of self-examination very seriously. If you're a Christian, yet you're still apathetic about your spiritual growth, then you haven't allowed God's Spirit to do his work in you. Ask yourself: are you growing more excited about Jesus and his church each day? Or do you still hold onto grudges, resentments, roots of bitterness, despite God's warnings? Are you growing spiritually, or has your growth been stunted?

It's possible for us to experience "exceeding growth" in many areas of our lives, and yet remain childish in one area. Paul says, "When I was a child, I spoke as a child, I understood as a child, I thought as a child: but when I became a man, I put away childish things" (1 Corinthians 13:11).

I challenge you to finish the following sentence: "My single biggest problem is..." (I wonder how your spouse or coworkers might fill in that blank!) Is your weakness flying off the handle? Is it pouting when things don't go your way? Are you a touchy, nagging spouse? Do you have a hard time forgiving someone for a hurt he caused you? Or is your problem a besetting lust or habit?

Some believers can tell you all about their spiritual growth, and you can clearly see the changes in their lives. They testify to you about how the Holy Ghost has vanquished the enemy for them, and you rejoice with them in their victory. Yet these Christians are the exception. Most believers are unaware of any spiritual progress in their lives. They're diligent to walk in holiness and in the fear of God. They pray, read the Bible and seek the Lord with all their hearts. They've forsaken all besetting lusts and habits. There's no obstruction to spiritual growth in them. In short, the life of Christ is thriving in these saints. But they can't discern any growth in themselves. They don't sense anything spiritual taking place at all. I'm an example of this type of Christian. I know I walk in the righteousness of Christ, yet I never feel holy or sense I'm making progress. In fact, I occasionally get down on myself whenever I do or say something un-Christlike. It causes me to wonder, "I've been a Christian for years. Why don't I ever learn?"

We all judge others to be so much purer and holier than ourselves. Yet we aren't aware of the wonderful, exceeding spiritual growth that God is causing in us!

I think the Thessalonian Christians were stunned when they heard Paul's glowing assessment of them. They probably thought, "Me, growing exceedingly? Paul must be kidding. Doesn't he know I'm still far from what I ought to be? On most days, I struggle badly. He may see growth in me, but I certainly don't."

Yet Paul knew that spiritual growth is a secret, hidden thing. Scripture likens it to the unseen growth of flowers and trees: "I will be as the dew unto Israel: he shall grow as the lily, and cast forth his roots as Lebanon. His branches shall spread, and his beauty shall be as the olive tree, and his smell as Lebanon" (Hosea 14:1-6). God is telling us, "Go to the lilies! Just try to watch them grow. Take your watch, and be prepared to stay all day long. I'm telling you, by day's end you won't be able to see any growth whatsoever. But know this: I water the lily every morning with the dew I send—and it's going to grow. Or, try to measure the growth of the cedar tree. Camp under it for a month, and tell me how far you see it grow. Even after six months, you probably won't notice any growth. Yet that tree is putting down deep roots! You see, I water the tree with my rain. And any tree that's watered properly is going to grow.

Yet such growth is not discernible to the human eye. It grows, but in secret!"

The same is true of most spiritual growth. It's imperceptible to the human eye!

Some Christians may object, "I've been a believer for ten years, and I still don't feel like I've grown spiritually." To those people, I point to the book of Isaiah. God promises, "I will pour water upon him that is thirsty, and floods upon the dry ground..." (Isaiah 44:3). He also calls his repentant people "trees of righteousness" (Isaiah 61:3). The Lord himself says we're his trees and flowers, his carefully tended plants. And he sends down his dew and rain upon us daily!

Let me give you an easy test that will reveal whether spiritual growth is taking place in you. Simply ask yourself, "Am I thirsty? Do I want more of Jesus and his holiness?" If the answer is yes, you can know you're growing. Why? He promises to pour out his living water on all who thirst for him: "Blessed are they which do hunger and thirst after righteousness: for they shall be filled" (Matthew 5:6). Simply put, God judges your spiritual growth by how much you hunger and thirst for him. So, if you're sincere about your walk with Christ, and you're open to his leading and correction, you mustn't be discouraged by any perceived lack of growth. True spiritual growth is taking place in you, whether you can see it or not! God promises that all who hunger and thirst after Him will be filled by His own hand. He'll water us from heaven. And He'll feed us all the nutrients needed to produce abundant life in us—whether we see it happening or not!

When some people get saved, they never again struggle with a besetting sin. They testify, "The moment I came to Jesus, the Lord took that temptation out of me. And I've been free ever since." I know many former drug addicts who've had this experience. They were saved in our ministry over the past thirty-five years, and they haven't had an addiction problem since. In fact, some serve as ministers and social workers today.

But for multitudes of Christians, it's a different story. Years after their conversion, they still battle a powerful, perplexing temptation. An old corruption has broken loose in them, something they hated and never wanted to see again. And that bondage is the one thing that's kept them from fullness in God. It brings guilt and reproach into their life. And if it were to be exposed, it could ruin them. Yet no matter how hard they struggle, that one remaining lust simply won't let go. Over time they grow discouraged. Their soul cries out, "How long, Lord? When will this chain ever be broken?" And eventually the devil comes to them, saying, "You'll never make it. Your sin is in you for good! You've struggled with this thing for years now. You know there's no way you could grow spiritually in this kind of condition."

Take heart, friend—I've got good news for you. You're growing in the midst of your struggle! In fact, you may be growing by leaps and bounds *because* of your struggle. Ask any sailor who's had to navigate through hurricanes and great storms. The waves may toss his ship around like a cork. The winds may shake the masts. The storm may even seem to push the ship backward. But even the most skilled sailor often can't discern whether his ship is making any headway. The same winds that threaten to take the ship down may actually be speeding it on its way!

Rest assured: if you have the fear of God in your heart, you're going to emerge from the storm much stronger. You see, when you're doing battle with the enemy, you're exercising and calling forth all the graces and powers of God. And even though you may feel weakened, those graces and powers are strengthening you. For one, you're becoming more urgent in your praying. And, second, you're being stripped of all pride. So, the storm is actually putting you on "spiritual guard" in every area of your life!

Whenever opposition arises, God's grace thrives in us. Think about what happens to a tree when a great storm beats violently against it. The wind threatens to uproot the tree and carry it away. It breaks off its branches and blows away its leaves. It loosens its roots and blows off its buds. And when the storm is over, things look utterly hopeless. Yet, look closer: the same storm that opened crevices in the earth around the trunk of the tree has helped the roots to go deeper. The tree now has access to new sources of nutrition and water, and it has been purged of all its dead branches. The buds may be gone, but others will grow back more fully. I tell you, that tree is now stronger, growing in unseen ways. And just wait till harvest, because it's going to bear much fruit!

Maybe you're in a storm right now. The wind is blowing hard, shaking you violently, and you think you're going down. Beloved, don't panic! You've got to know that in the midst of the tempest, you're putting down deep spiritual roots. God is developing in you a deepening humility, a greater mourning and sorrow for sin, a heightened hunger for his righteousness.

Other Christians who haven't known spiritual warfare may look down their noses at their brothers and sisters who struggle in ways they don't. But you no longer have that attitude. Now, because of your own struggles, you're more tenderhearted toward the weaknesses and failings of others. Though you haven't been aware of it, the Lord has used the storm to deepen in you the roots of Christ's compassion. In short, God is making you a seasoned soldier of the cross—battle-scarred, but battle-smart and courageous. You may get down on yourself at times, but the Lord never does. The fact is, He could have acted sovereignly at any time to pluck you out of your struggle. But He didn't, because He saw it producing in you a greater thirst for Him!

Think about it all: your new humility, your new sorrow for sin, your new hunger for Christ; none of these things was present in you when you weren't engaged in spiritual warfare. Now you're growing ever stronger, in spite of your ongoing battle. You've resisted by faith alone. And although you've stumbled, you always get back up and return to the cross. You're holding onto a promise of covenant power. And in the process, you're growing holier, more humble—more like Jesus! Yet the devil wants to convince you that your sin-struggle proves you're wicked and hell-bound. No; he's a liar! And he has trapped countless Christians with this hellish lie!

Scripture says that God will not break a bruised reed. Do you want to grow spiritually? If so, ask the Holy Ghost to shine his light on your one area of weakness or sin. And cry out to him, "Lord, I want to measure up to your word. And I know only you have the power to accomplish that in me. Please, help me to grasp by faith that you're at work in me, growing me up spiritually!"

God wants you to know that right now, in the midst of your storm, He stands beside you. He's watering your spirit, feeding your soul, putting down His strong roots in you. Let the winds of struggle blow hard. Your Father is preparing you for a great harvest!

As we read the words of David in Psalm 38, we find this godly, righteous man at the end of himself. He was downcast and discouraged, and his struggle had drained him of all strength. Listen to his distraught cry: "I am troubled; I am bowed down greatly; I go mourning all the day long. I am feeble and sore broken: I have roared by reason of the disquietness of my heart. My heart panteth, my strength faileth me: as for the light of mine eyes, it also is gone from me. I, as a deaf man, heard not; and I was as a dumb man that openeth not his mouth. Thus I was as a man that heareth not, and in whose mouth are no reproofs" (Psalm 38:6, 8, 10, 13-14)."

As I read this Psalm, I imagine David slumped in despair. Perhaps what troubled him most was that he couldn't understand why he was suddenly cast down so low. This man hungered for the Lord, pouring out his heart daily in prayer. He revered God's word, writing Psalms that extolled his glory. But now, in his depressed state, all he could do was cry, "Lord, I'm at the end of my rope. And I have no idea why it's happening!"

Like many discouraged Christians today, David tried to figure out why he felt so empty and broken in spirit. He probably relived every failure, sin, and foolish deed in his life. At some point he must have thought, "Oh, Lord, have all my reckless acts left me so wounded that I'm beyond hope?" Finally, David reasoned that God must have been chastening him. He cried, "O Lord, rebuke me not in thy wrath: neither chasten me in thy hot displeasure. For thine arrows stick fast in me, and thy hand presseth me sore. There is no soundness in my flesh because of thine anger; neither is there any rest in my bones because of my sin. For mine iniquities are gone over my head: as an heavy burden they are too heavy for me" (Psalm 38: 1-4).

Let me point out here that David isn't just writing about his own condition in this Psalm. He's describing something that all devoted lovers of Jesus face at some point in their lifetime. He's talking about being under a demonic attack from a plaguing spirit of discouragement! This kind of discouraging spirit comes straight from the bowels of hell. And the time comes when every dedicated believer is overwhelmed by this sudden and unexpected experience. No Christian brings it on himself, nor does the Lord send it. Such an attack usually has nothing to do with any specific sin or failing by the believer.

Very simply, the spirit of discouragement is Satan's most potent weapon against God's elect. Most often, he uses it to try to convince us that we've brought God's wrath upon ourselves by not measuring up to His holy standards. But the Apostle Paul urges us not to fall prey to the devil's snare. "Lest Satan should get an advantage of us: for we are not ignorant of his devices" (2 Corinthians 2:11).

Paul is saying, "You have to see your discouragement for what it really is! It's a demonic weapon, an arrow that Satan shoots at you from his quiver to get you to doubt yourself. He knows he can't tempt you to turn away from Jesus. So he swamps you with vicious lies to make you think you'll never be good enough to serve Christ. He wants to get you so downcast that you'll want to throw in the towel!"

Feebleness, soreness, brokenness, troubles, disquietness, mourning; all of these things bowed David's spirit low. He felt dry and empty, without direction, as if he'd learned nothing over the years. "As for the light of mine eyes, it also is gone from me" (Psalm 38:10). David is saying, "I've lost my spiritual understanding. My vision and revelation of the Lord have left me. I can't reach God as I used to!"

I know just how David felt. My life has been full of such rich blessings. But often, I end up thinking, "Lord, my life has been a complete waste. I haven't accomplished anything for you!" That's the work of Satan's spirit of discouragement. It makes us a target for the powers of Hell within moments of our greatest spiritual victory!

This heavy, demonic spirit laid David so low, he was dumbfounded in God's presence. He said, "But I, as a deaf man, heard not; and I was as a dumb man that openeth not his mouth. Thus I was as a man that heareth not, and in whose mouth are no reproofs" (Psalm 38: 13-14). The Hebrew meaning of this last phrase is a man who has no more answers or arguments left. David was saying, "Lord, I'm too down and discouraged to even lift my hand up to you. I can't pray, because I'm too confused to speak. I'm drained and empty. I have nothing to say."

David's trial was not at all unique. I've read many biographies of devout men and women whom the Lord used mightily, and every one of these people struggled through the same kind of crippling discouragement. David voiced the universal cry of the righteous soul that endures an attack of discouragement: "I am ready to halt, and my sorrow is continually before me" (Psalm 38: 17). The word "halt" here, in Hebrew, means "fall." David was telling God, "I'm not going to make it, Lord. I'm at my absolute end and I'm about to fall!"

We can talk to God all we want about our feelings of failure. We can tell him about our despair over our sins and foolish mistakes. But we are never to entertain the thought that he has abandoned us. This is a serious accusation, and our Lord doesn't take it lightly. We see his immediate response to this kind of accusation in Numbers: "(Israel) journeyed from mount Hor by the way of the Red Sea...and the soul of the people was much discouraged because of the way. And the people spake against God, and against Moses, Wherefore have ye brought us up out of Egypt to die in the wilderness? For there is no bread, neither is there any water; and our soul loatheth this light bread; and the Lord sent fiery serpents among the people, and they bit the people; and much people of Israel died" (Numbers 21:4-6).

When the Bible tells me my loving heavenly father sent fiery serpents upon his own people, and that they died from the snake bites, I can't ignore the very clear message: God will not allow such unbelief among his elect! After all that our precious Lord has done for us, the most hurtful accusation we can make against him is that he has neglected us. We are to beware of such unbelief, especially in our difficult times. David is our example of someone who kept his faith. Even at his lowest point, David wouldn't allow himself to wallow in unbelief. He cried, "For in thee, O Lord, do I hope: thou wilt hear, O Lord my God" (Psalm 38:15).

If you're enduring an attack from a demonic spirit of discouragement, I suggest that you not try to escape the attack through your own wits. You're no match for the demonic spirit you're up against. The battle is far beyond your human skill or physical power to wage. Nor can you merely talk it out with friends, or try to overcome it through books, seminars, or counselors. The conflict is in the spiritual realm, and it has to be fought in the spirit.

In his time of discouragement, David couldn't figure out why he was so cast down. He asked, "Why art thou cast down, O my soul? And why art thou disquieted in me?" (Psalm 42:5). Yet his questions weren't doubts about God. David actually begins the psalm by expressing his deep thirst for the Lord: "As the hart [deer] panteth after the water brooks, so panteth my soul after thee, O God. My soul thirsteth for God, for the living God: when shall I come and appear before God?" (Psalm 42:1-2).

In the midst of his discouragement, David cried out for a revelation of the Lord. He was saying, "God, there's never been a time when I've loved you more. I thirst for you like the running deer who pants for water. So why am I so cast down? Why am I suffering such overwhelming discouragement?"

Of course, at times David experienced despair and depression because of his sin. He endured the Lord's chastening for his pride when he numbered his fighting men, which was against God's law. And he felt the pain of God's rod when he committed adultery with Bathsheba and arranged to have her husband murdered. His heart broke with dejection over the judgment he brought on his family because of these sins.

So, too, many believers today are discouraged because of their sins. Some are depressed because the Holy Spirit has wanted to bring them into victory, but they resist. They've chosen the way of the flesh, and that always leads to pain and discouragement.

However, I'm addressing repentant believers here, those who seek God with all their hearts. These faithful servants are gripped by a different kind of discouragement. This kind comes upon them suddenly, out of nowhere, for no apparent reason. And it totally dumbfounds them.

If this is true of you, you can be absolutely sure you are under attack! Satan has sent a cloud of discouragement to overwhelm you. And he has his reasons for doing so! You see, discouragement is the devil's most devastating tool in his attacks on Spirit-hungry saints. It has been the enemy's weapon of choice for centuries against God's elect. From the day you became serious about the things of God, determining in your heart to know Christ in his fullness, Satan has sought to discourage you. He has watched you dig deeper into God's Word every day. He has seen you changing, growing, overcoming all worldliness. So he has made you a target for heavy attack. And you'd better believe that attack will come!

Right now, you may be able to praise God loudly in church, saying, "This is the greatest day of joy I've ever had!" But watch out for what comes tomorrow. Satan will use his most powerful weapon, discouragement, to try to bring you down. However, when the attack comes, don't think it's unusual. God allows this kind of fiery testing with all his saints! Peter writes, "Beloved, think it not strange concerning the fiery trial which is to try you, as though some strange thing happened unto you" (1 Peter 4:12). Discouragement is a trial God's people have endured for centuries!

When you're under attack from the enemy's spirit of discouragement, you won't feel like praying. But you must still go to the secret place and be in Jesus' presence. You don't need to worry about trying to pray your way out of despair. This is the time for God's Spirit to go to work in you. It's his job to lift you out of the pit.

When you go to the Lord, be honest with him. Tell him how weak and helpless you feel. Let him know, "Jesus, I'm dry. I have no strength left. If I'm ever going to get out of this depression, you're going to have to make it happen." In such low times, the Lord is very patient with us. He doesn't expect us to exert some intense, fervent effort in prayer. He knows our condition, and he sympathizes with us. So, just sit in his presence and trust his Spirit to do in you what he has been sent to do. It doesn't matter how cast down you are; he will never forsake you!

We have the notion that every time we fail the Lord, the Holy Ghost flits away like a bird. Some Puritan divines taught this. They believed that God's Spirit leaves Christians for a season whenever he's grieved with them. I could never understand or accept this doctrine. How could God's Spirit abandon me when I need him most? If he leaves me whenever I fail and fall deep into discouragement, how could he be my comforter? That wouldn't provide any comfort at all. In fact, it would leave me in Satan's power! Likewise, if the Holy Ghost is my soul's sanctifier, how could he do this work if he flies in and out of my life every time I fail? How could I ever see my sin without the Spirit's presence there to convict me of it? How could I know how to change if he wasn't there to guide and direct me?

Jesus promised us, "I will pray the Father, and he shall give you another Comforter, that he may abide with you for ever. I will not leave you comfortless: I will come to you" (John 14:16, 18).

When the devil's heavy spirit of discouragement settles over your life, you may be so distraught you can't even whisper a prayer. But even if you can't utter a word, you can talk to Jesus in your spirit. Just tell him softly, "Lord, help me. This attack is too much for me. I can't do anything but sit here in faith. I'm trusting your Spirit to drive it out of me." As Jesus said, "The Comforter, which is the Holy Ghost, whom the Father will send in my name, He shall teach you all things, and bring all things to your remembrance, whatsoever I have said unto you" (John 14:26).

When the devil comes with his spirit of discouragement, he bombards you with one lie after another. He lies to you about your marriage, your family, your friendships, your calling, your walk with the Lord. Then he begins to replay in your mind every sin, failure and foolish thing you've ever done. By the time he's finished, you're crying, "Oh, God I'll never make it!" The first thing the Holy Spirit does in such times is to bring to your remembrance all the precious promises of Jesus. The best is still ahead of you.

That is the work of the Holy Spirit. He undoes the lies of the enemy, and brings encouragement from on high!

Many Christians enter God's presence every day expecting to be reproved by him. How that must grieve our Lord! When we go to prayer, we ought to be prepared to hear a good word from our loving father. But many believers rarely are. Be assured, all who wait on the Lord will receive his glorious promises:

- "Since the beginning of the world men have not heard, nor perceived by the ear, neither hath the eye seen, O God, beside thee, what he hath prepared for him that waiteth for him" (Isaiah 64:4).

- "As it is written, Eye hath not seen, nor ear heard, neither have entered into the heart of man, the things which God hath prepared for them that love him. But God hath revealed them unto us by his Spirit: for the Spirit searcheth all things, yea, the deep things of God" (1 Corinthians 2:9-10).

Let's take a closer look at two phrases from the passage in Corinthians:

1. "The things which God hath prepared for them that love him" (Verse 9). Satan can attack you, flooding you with lies and discouraging words. But if you'll simply wait on the Lord, his Spirit will come to you in the midst of the attack and drive out all the devil's lies. How? He'll give you a revelation of all the good things God has prepared for you because you love him! Our Lord has a wonderful plan for every single child who loves him. And no satanic attack against his children can ever alter those plans. God knows the sorrows, struggles and pain we may be facing today. But he also knows the glorious things he has laid out ahead of us. He knows the revelation we'll receive, the usefulness we'll enjoy, the fruit we'll see, the joy and peace we'll possess. He has a good word for all who love him!

2. "God hath revealed them unto us by his Spirit" (Verse 10). The Lord desires to show us his Good Word about what he has prepared for us. And his Spirit is the messenger who bears that Good Word. The Holy Ghost will give wings to our drooping spirits with God's revelation to us, and we'll fly like eagles out of Satan's snare!

Listen to these wonderful words from Isaiah:

"Hast thou not known? Hast thou not heard, that the everlasting God, the Lord, the Creator of the ends of the Earth, fainteth not, neither is weary? There is no searching of his understanding. He giveth power to the faint; and to them that have no might he increaseth strength. Even the youths shall faint and be weary, and the young men shall utterly fall: but they that wait on the Lord shall renew their strength; they shall mount up with wings as eagles; they shall run, and not be weary; and they shall walk, and not faint" (Isaiah 40:28-31). That is the work of the Holy Spirit: to encourage us. Our work is simply to trust him to fulfill what the Father has sent him to do.

Go to your secret closet right now, even in your discouraged state, and quiet yourself before the Lord. Even if you don't have strength enough to speak, you can reach out to him in Spirit. Say to him this prayer:

"Lord, I know your Spirit abides in me. And I know you've sent him to comfort me, strengthen me, and reveal the mind of Christ to me. So, Holy Ghost, I turn to you right now in simple, childlike faith. Speak to my heart your words of comfort. I don't have any strength left. You're going to have to lift me up and lead me."

The Spirit of Christ won't let you be deceived. He'll show you the good things God has ahead for you. But you must dare to believe he will speak to you!

You're not going to faint. You're going to come out of your trial more victorious, because your faith will have been tested and tried as gold. And you'll see the Lord fulfill every promise he has made to you.

Back Page Summary

For many of us, sinking to the bottom means the end; and we become so overwhelmed by our failures and our successes that we sometimes develop a sense of unworthiness. Have you been there? I've been trapped at times beyond human help, but Jesus Christ was there all the time. I too have made that midnight cry, "Lord Jesus Christ, where are you when I need you? It's Oscar! I need deliverance! Where are you? I've done everything I know and called everybody I thought might lend me a hand—yet I'm still not free. I'm sick and tired of repenting and crying out without seeing any change... Where are you, God? Have you forgotten about me?"

The fact is, this book reveals The Divine Advocate, who is there to present our claim by asking in His Name; and now our case belongs to Him. Our humble, simple prayer becomes His prayer at God's right hand. I have literally dropped out of the question, and the Mighty Advocate takes over my case.

Today, I challenge my mountain in that all-sufficient Name of God...and it must move.

We must become Scriptural Believers, each a child of God, obeying His Word.

The Name of Jesus Christ is great.

He has given us legal authority to use His Name.

He has given us Power of Attorney, which is identical with the presence of the person who gave it to us.

Thank you for staying with me and taking time to read this book. I encourage you to review and really ponder the truths shared here. It has been a sacrifice, along with years of study, trying to bring this to you from my heart. Just know that he is not "Hidden" any longer. We are positioned with Him in His kingdom, and we have been instructed to spread the news of His Kingdom whereever we go, that others may choose to be part of His kingdom also.

How hungry are you for a FRESH Manifestation of His Presence?

Special Edition Message: Enjoy Life As God Intended

To: *He Came Incognito*
By Oscar Smith
2013 09 03

ADotComChurch.com The response to this Church has been very gratifying as people all over the world have stopped by to read our messages and grow stronger in faith and closer in their relationship with our wonderful Lord Jesus Christ. We are thrilled with Jesus Christ. It is my belief that everyone would love Him if they just knew Him. My quest is to help you know Him and His Word better. Before you begin reading this Special Edition, I suggest you ask the Lord Jesus to open your understanding and teach you. It is always a good idea to approach God's Word with a request for God's help.

Although my writings in this book are not perfect as I never pursued a scholarly work (because I don't know everything yet), I trust they will point you to the One who is perfect — Lord Jesus Christ — and His Word. And that through Jesus Christ you will enjoy life as God intended. God anoints His people for very specific purposes and we must sometimes wait on the anointing to give us direction. Our own desires can frustrate and misdirect. I operate in the office of a Chaplain and teacher and it has not been easy but I've stayed with what I know God has called and anointed me to do.

Now I know for a fact that there are many who have billed themselves as apostles, bishops, doctors and prophets prematurely. This could be what Paul had in mind when he said that people should not think more highly of themselves than they ought to think. If that kind of calling and anointing is upon a minister, others will be aware of it. They will not have to advertise or self - promote with man- made titles. I have absolutely refused to try being someone else which causes nothing but frustration in the Body of Christ. Stay and trust the anointing God has placed on your life. (1 Corinthians 2:4-6) Draw from God's wisdom.

Compromise elsewhere but please never compromise your God given anointing. Being a Christian is being united with Jesus, a member of His body, with His life in your heart. Jesus should be your focus — not religious activity — but the person of Jesus, the Lord and Christ.

He Came Incognito "In Jesus'" Confessions:

In Jesus I reign in life (Rom. 5:17).

In Jesus I walk in newness of life (Rom. 6:4).

In Jesus I am alive unto God (Rom. 6:11).

In Jesus I bring forth fruits unto God (Rom. 7:4).

In Jesus I have no condemnation (Rom. 8:1).

In Jesus I have been made free from the law of sin and death (Rom. 8:2).

In Jesus I live by the law of the Spirit of life (Rom. 8:2).

In Jesus I am a child of God (Rom. 8:16).

In Jesus I am an heir of God (Rom. 8:17).

In Jesus I am a joint-heir with Christ (Rom. 8:17).

In Jesus I freely receive all things from God (Rom. 8:32).

In Jesus I am more than a conqueror (Rom. 8:37).

In Jesus nothing can separate me from the love of God (Rom. 8:38-39).

In Jesus I am sanctified (1 Cor. 1:2).

In Jesus I am enriched in all knowledge (1 Cor. 1:5).

In Jesus I have wisdom (1 Cor. 1:30).

In Jesus I have righteousness (1 Cor. 1:30).

In Jesus I have sanctification (1 Cor. 1:30).

In Jesus I have redemption (1 Cor. 1:30).

In Jesus I shall be resurrected (1 Cor. 15:20-22).

In Jesus I have victory over death (1 Cor. 15:57).

In Jesus all the promises of God are "Yes" and "Amen" to me (2 Cor. 1:20).

In Jesus I am established (2 Cor. 1:21).

In Jesus I am anointed of God (2 Cor. 1:21).

In Jesus I always triumph (2 Cor. 2:14).

In Jesus I am a sweet fragrance to God (2 Cor. 2:15).

In Jesus my mind is renewed and enlightened (2 Cor. 3:14).

In Jesus I am a new creature (2 Cor. 5:17).

In Jesus I have the ministry of reconciliation (2 Cor. 5:18).

In Jesus I am an ambassador for God (2 Cor. 5:20).

In Jesus I am made the righteousness of God (2 Cor. 5:21).

In Jesus I live by the power of God (2 Cor. 13:4).

In Jesus I have liberty (Gal. 2:4).

In Jesus I am redeemed from the curse of the law (Gal. 3:13).

In Jesus I have the blessing of Abraham (Gal. 3:14).

In Jesus I am a son of God (Gal. 4:7).

In Jesus I have faith which works by love (Gal. 5:6).

In Jesus I am blessed with all spiritual blessings in heavenly places (Eph. 1:3).

In Jesus I have been chosen before the foundation of the world (Eph. 1:4).

In Jesus I am accepted of God (Eph. 1:6).

In Jesus I have the life of God (Eph. 2:5).

In Jesus I now sit in heavenly places (Eph. 2:6).

In Jesus I have the exceeding riches of God's grace and kindness (Eph. 2:7).

In Jesus I am His workmanship (Eph. 2:10).

In Jesus I am created for good works (Eph. 2:10).

In Jesus I am built together for a habitation of God through the Spirit (Eph. 2:22).

In Jesus I have boldness and access with confidence before God (Eph. 3:12).

In Jesus I am a shining light (Eph. 5:8).

In Jesus I am strong in the power of God's might (Eph. 6:10).

In Jesus I have the high calling of God (Phil. 3:14).

In Jesus I do not worry (Phil 4:6).

In Jesus I have the peace of God which passes all understanding (Phil. 4:7).

In Jesus I have the peace of God which guards my heart and mind (Phil. 4:7).

In Jesus I have strength (Phil. 4:13).

In Jesus I can do all things (Phil. 4:13).

In Jesus all my needs are met according to God's riches in glory (Phil. 4:19).

In Jesus I have been delivered from the power of darkness (Col. 1:13).

In Jesus I have been translated into the kingdom of God (Col. 1:13).

In Jesus I have redemption through His blood (Col. 1:14).

In Jesus I have forgiveness of sins (Col. 1:14).

In Jesus I am reconciled to God (Col. 1:20).

In Jesus I have all the treasures of wisdom and knowledge (Col. 2:3).

In Jesus I am made complete and perfect (Col. 2:10).

In Jesus my life is hid with Him in God (Col. 3).

In Jesus I have abundant love (1 Tim. 1:14).

In Jesus I have obtained salvation with eternal glory (2 Tim. 2:10).

In Jesus I am saved to the uttermost (Heb. 7:25).

In Jesus I have eternal redemption (Heb. 9:12).

In Jesus I have an eternal inheritance (Heb. 9:12).

In Jesus I am made perfect in every good work to do His will (Heb. 13:21).

In Jesus I have abundant mercy from God (1 Peter 1:3).

In Jesus I have a lively hope (1 Peter 1:3).

In Jesus I have joy unspeakable (1 Peter 1:8).

In Jesus I am a holy priest of God (1 Peter 2:5).

In Jesus I am settled (1 Peter 5:10).

In Jesus I have fellowship with all believers (1 John 1:7).

In Jesus I have received the anointing which teaches me all things (1 John 2:27).

In Jesus I have the Spirit of God (1 John 3:24).

In Jesus I have overcome the devil, the flesh and the world (1 John 4:4).

In Jesus God dwells in me (1 John 4:15).

In Jesus I have the love of God (1 John 4:16).

In Jesus I have no fear (1 John 4:18).

In Jesus I overcome the world (1 John 5:4).

In Jesus I have victory (1 John 5:4).

In Jesus I have understanding (1 John 5:20). In Jesus I know God (1 John 5:20).

(1 CORINTHIANS 1:9) God has called you into fellowship with his Son Jesus Christ our Lord who is faithful. Church meetings, Bible reading, etc. can be good, but should not be allowed to become an end all be all. They are tools to help us know Jesus and walk more closely with Him. The Bible says we are to be faithful; but faithful to what: a religious system, an organization — or, a Person? Are you serving Jesus — or serving something else as His substitute? The focus of our life should be to please Lord Jesus Christ. COLOSSIANS 1:18 He is the head of the body, the church; he is the beginning, the firstborn from the dead, so that he might come to have first place in everything. Does Jesus have first place in your life? In everything, Jesus should be our central focus. He wants all of our tomorrows, the Lord appeared to Abraham one day and gave him an incredible command: "Get thee out of thy country, and from thy kindred, and from thy father's house, unto a land that I will show

thee" (Genesis 12:1). What an amazing thing. Suddenly, God picked out a man and told him, "I want you to get up and go, leaving everything behind: your home, your relatives, even your country. I want to send you someplace, and I will direct you how to get there along the way." How did Abraham respond to this incredible word from the Lord? "By faith Abraham, when he was called to go out into a place which he should after receive for an inheritance, obeyed; and he went out, not knowing whither he went" (Hebrews 11:8). What was God up to? Why would he search the nations for one man, and then call him to forsake everything and go on a journey with no map, no preconceived direction, with no known destination? Think about what God was asking of Abraham. He never showed him how he would feed or support his family. He didn't tell him how far to go or when he would arrive. He only told him two things in the beginning: "Go," and, "I will show you the way." In essence, God told Abraham, "From this day on, I want you to give me all your tomorrows. You're to live the rest of your life putting your future into my hands, one day at a time. I'm asking you to commit your life to a promise that I am making to you, Abraham. If you will commit to do this, I will bless you, guide you and lead you to a place you never imagined."

The place God wanted to lead Abraham is a place he wants to take every member of Christ's body. Abraham is what Bible scholars call a "pattern man," someone who serves as an example of how to walk before the Lord. Abraham's example shows us what is required of all who would seek to please God.

Please make no mistake Abraham was not a young man when God called him to make this commitment. He probably had plans in place to secure his family's future, so he had to be concerned over many considerations as he weighed God's call. Yet Abraham "believed in the Lord; and [God] counted it to him for righteousness" (Genesis 15:6).

The apostle Paul tells us that all who believe and trust in Christ are the children of Abraham. And, like Abraham, we are counted as righteous because we heed the same call to entrust all our tomorrows into the Lord's hands.

Our Wonderful God Has Not Fainted and He Never Will.

"Have you not known? Have you not heard?

The everlasting God, the Lord, the Creator of

the ends of the earth neither faints nor is weary.

There is no searching of His understanding (Isaiah 40:28).

There is an ignorance of God that supposes He no longer reveals Himself to mankind in his crises and needs that He is dead or asleep, he is unable to monitor or direct the steps of man. But who is man or woman to measure God? To whom will we compare Him to?

 Have you not known?

Have you not heard?

The everlasting Creator,

The God of the ends of the world,

Neither slumbers nor sleeps.

He faints not,

Neither is weary,

But they that trust in Him

Shall renew their faith and strength

They shall fly as eagles:

They shall run and not be weary,

Nor shall they faint.

I have given my lifeblood to this work and I know from first had experience that only one thing conquers and dispels darkness, and that is light. Isaiah declared, "The people that walked in darkness have seen a great light" (Isaiah 9:2). Likewise, John stated, "The light shines in darkness; and the darkness comprehended it not" (John 1:5). Light represents understanding. When we say, "I see the light," we're saying, now I understand. Do you see what Scripture is saying? The Lord is about to open our eyes, not to see a victorious devil but to receive new revelation. Our God has sent us his Holy Ghost, whose power is greater than all the powers of hell: "Greater is he that is in you, than he that is in the world" (1 John 4:4). In Revelation we read of hell spewing forth locusts and scorpions that have great power. We read of a dragon, beasts, horned creatures, as well as a coming Antichrist. Yet, we don't know the meaning of all these creatures. That is, we don't have to. We don't need to worry about the Antichrist or the mark of the beast. There is living in us the Spirit of Almighty God and his Christ. Paul declares that the power of the Holy Spirit is working in us. In other words, the Holy Ghost is alive in us at this very moment. So, how does the Spirit work in us in the midst of hard times? His power is released only as we receive him as our burden bearer. The Holy Spirit was given to us for this very reason, to bear our cares and worries. So, how can we say we've received him if we haven't turned over our burdens to him?

The Holy Spirit isn't shut up in glory, but is here, abiding in us. And he's waiting anxiously to take control of every situation in our lives, including our afflictions. So, if we continue in fear—despairing, questioning, going deeper into anxiety—then we haven't received him as our comforter, helper, guide, rescuer and strength.

The witness to the world is the Christian who has cast his every burden on the Holy Spirit. As I sit here this morning Marsha and I having breakfast we are fully trusting God's Spirit for our comfort and for guidance out of our afflictions. My wife Marsha and I have a powerful testimony to a lost world, because we embody joy despite being surrounded by darkness. His life in us is not hidden and it tells the world, we are a family that has seen the light. When Adam sinned, he tried to hide from God. When Peter denied Christ, he was afraid to face him. When Jonah refused to preach to Nineveh, his fear drove him into the ocean, to flee the presence of the Lord. Something much worse than failure is the fear that goes with it. Adam, Jonah, and Peter ran away from God, not because they lost their love for him, but because they were afraid he was too angry with them to understand. The accuser of the brethren waits, like a vulture, for you to fail in some way. Then he uses every lie in hell to make you give up or convince you that God is too Holy or you are too sinful to come back. Or he makes you afraid you are not perfect enough or that you will never rise above your failure. It took forty years to get the fear out of Moses and to make him usable in God's program. If Moses or Jacob or David had resigned himself to failure, we might never again have heard of these men. Yet Moses rose up again to become one of God's greatest heroes.

Jacob faced his sins, was reunited with the brother he had cheated, and reached new heights of victory. David ran into the house of God, found forgiveness and peace, and returned to his finest hour. Jonah retraced his steps, did what he had refused to do at first and brought a whole city to repentance. Peter rose out of the ashes of denial to lead a church to Pentecost. Just a few days ago I sat in our little sunroom alone weeping; Oscar, Chap Oscar you're a terrible failure, your writing and releasing a second edition is totally foolish. I shudder to think of how many blessings Marsha and I would miss if we give up in this dark hour. How glad I am just three days later thanking God who encouraged me to face my doubts and go on to His next step for me.

Here Are the Wonderful Names of Jesus

- "Jesus"

- "Christ"

- "Lord"

- "Jesus Christ"

- "Christ Jesus"

- "Son of Man"

- "Son of God"

We must stay sheltered in the calm of God. Jesus Chris draws upon the wisdom of His Father God. At this Hour we too must learn to remain calm, we must learn to wait, and listen to hear the voice of Our Father. This is the pattern for true discernment: we disown the limits of our opinions and reactions, and we learn to wait and listen to the Lord. When we accept Christ into our hearts, He does not enter simply as a doctrine. No, He enters us as a living voice. His Spirit brings conviction and direction; He speaks through dreams, visions, revelation, and understanding of the Scriptures. He illuminates our hearts, speaking to us of repentance and the renewal of our soul. He lifts us, reminding us of the faithful promises of God. Yet this voice - the sacred voice of God - refuses to compete with the clamor of our fleshly minds. This is God, King and Creator of the universe. He requires the honor of our full attention. He will not yell as though we were disobedient children He will not chase us, He waits. There are times when He may resist us, gently pushing against our prideful efforts. He will wait until we stop our harmful activity. Our problem is not that God won't come to us; it's that our anxious souls fail to give Him time to speak. Remember, His thoughts are "higher than" our thoughts (Isa. 55:9). He would speak to us, but sometimes our opinions monopolize the conversation.

Our ideas and preprogrammed reactions rush out of our mouths and into the world of men. We hurry by the narrow path that leads to His presence. He is left out of the conversation; He wants in, "Take care what you listen to" (Mark 4:24).

As the World's Most Loved Chaplain according to my friend Mr. Quantum Ted Ciuba it is my humble opinion that the Future of our world is based 100 % on the awesome Power locked up in Forgiveness! Perhaps nothing so typifies the transforming, cleansing power of God as that which is experienced when a soul receives forgiveness. It is the power of new life, of new hopes and of new joy. It is the river of life flowing again into the cold, hardened valleys of a once-embittered heart. Forgiveness is the essence of revival itself. Whenever pardon is given there is a dramatic release of life, not only between those once estranged, but also there is an increase of life in the heavenly places. Observe the release of power when Jesus prayed "Father, forgive them . . ." (Luke 23:34). At that very moment every demonic principality and power which had infiltrated man's relationship with God was legally "...disarmed!" (Col 2:15) As Christ pleaded, ". . . they know not what they do," hell's gates began to unlock, soon tombs opened, the veil into the holy place rent, and heaven itself opened -- all because of Jesus' forgiveness!

Consider the last time you experienced full healing in a severed relationship. It is likely such words as "wonderful" and "glorious" were used to describe the baptism of love that renewed your souls. Can we see that forgiveness is the very heart of Christ's message?

Forgiveness is the very spirit of heaven removing the hiding places of demonic activity from the caverns of the human soul. It is every wrong made right and every evil made void. The power released in forgiveness is actually a mighty weapon. Darkness is certainly coming, and judgment is at our very door. But as God's people, we cannot allow any cloud of darkness to hide the light of his great promises of love and mercy toward his people. We are to be well informed by the Lord's words and prophets, but we are not to dwell on prophetic knowledge so much that it takes over our lives. How quickly we forget God's great deliverances in our lives. How easily we take for granted the miracles he performed in our lives. Yet the Bible tells us over and over, "Remember your deliverances." We're so like the disciples. They didn't understand Christ's miracles when he supernaturally fed thousands with just a few loaves and fishes. We have absolute access to the very presence of the Creator, the living God!

He Came Incognito Love

by Oscar Smith

The measure of our Love is the measure of our worth.

We have never thought of it in these terms but many are valued according to their financial or political standing in a community. Yet, in the final analysis, the people who love are the people who help the community. We were created by love to answer the heart cry of the God. Living outside of love makes us a failure. Selfishness is a curse to the human family. Love stops the rust of selfishness, preserves the home and Church life from decay. Love is like rust-proof steel. Love is Gods adhesive that keep us together.

> Love never fails. It is the Master-ruler.
> It will lead a man out of selfishness, out of weakness and failure into the very strength and ability of Christ.
> There is no force in the world that it cannot dominate.
> It makes us wanted.
> It makes us a blessing.
> It enables us to take Jesus' place.
> I have sometimes wondered what would happen if we all dared to go to the limit with Love.
> Love must be enthroned in the heart.
> It must govern our life.
> As love takes over the kingdom of our spirit, then that wonderful passage in II Corinthians 5:14-15 becomes a living reality: " For the love of Christ constrain us because we thus judge, that one died for all, therefore all died; and he died for all, that I whom he has made alive, should no longer live unto myself but unto Him who for our sakes died and rose again."

Selfishness is as deadly poison.
It is poison to the spirit.
It is poison to the Body of Christ.
It causes practically all the diseases in the body.
It is a strange thing how selfishness has never been feared by man.
He fears it in the other man but not in himself.

That thing born in the Garden has grown so mighty that it governs the nations of the earth, and Love is the only thing that can destroy it.
1 John 4:16 was one of the hardest Scriptures that ever faced me.
It didn't seem to me that I could ever enter into it.
God is love; and he that abides in love abides in God and God in him."
First, I have come to believe in Love.
I believe it is best to let love govern my life.

Walk the Love way, and when we do, we discover we are living in the Love Realm. Our home is filled with Love. Whenever we step out of Love, we step into darkness and unhappiness, and so Marsha and I have learned to stay in the Love way. We have found that living in Love is actually living in the highest, sweetest fellowship with the Father.
It is actually living with Him.
He has come into us!

The One Great Subject of the Word which runs through the whole Word of God is Jesus Christ: the promised seed of the woman in Gen. 3:15. This verse marks the depth of the ruin into which man had descended in the Fall and it becomes the foundation of the rest of the Bible. All hope of restoration for man and for creation is centered in Christ; who in due time should be born into the world, should suffer and die; and, in resurrection, should become the Head of a new creation. Hence, Christ, "the Coming One," is the one all-pervading subject of the Word of God as a whole. He is the life giving spirit of the written Word, without which the latter is dead. "As the body without life is dead" (Jas. 2:26), so the written Word without life is dead also. Christ is that life or Spirit. This is absolutely a great time to be alive especially for those of us who love Lord Jesus Christ. The opportunities are unparalleled with the millions of searching hearts and agonized souls. AdotcomChurch.com is on the forefront of an emerging revolution as there is no returning to the old ways of doing Church. We are an extensive grassroots response to the undeniable longing for a genuine relationship with God our Father. We are involved with a wide variety of activities and connections like Ted Ciuba's ThinkRichRadio.com with Chap Oscar as Co-Host broadcast weekly to a global audience. AdotcomChurch.com has no single leader and no headquarters. Our Declaration of Purpose is more than two thousand years old: the Bible. The world is our Church grounds and everyone we meet is a soul to love into the permanent presence and experience of God.

There is no greater calling than to know and serve God. Marsha and I live and want nothing more than to hear God say to each one of us "Well done, my good and faithful servants." At AdotcomChurch.com Christ, and Christ alone, is the center of life and worship. He is the head of the body, the Church: who is the beginning, the firstborn from the dead; that in all things He might have the pre-eminence. For it pleased the Father that in Him should all fullness dwell (Col. 1:18-19) "That in all things He might have the pre-eminence That is - distinguished and spoken of above all others. Having first place in all things, not even the Holy Spirit is to be exalted above His name. The upper room must never overshadow the Cross! We dare not think of Christ as simply the one who sent the Holy Spirit. In other words, "Thank You, Jesus, for sending someone better." Christ sent the Holy Spirit to reveal His own fullness within us. When the Holy Spirit becomes the center of our attention, the church gets out of focus. The Holy Spirit descended upon Christ as He came out of baptismal waters, and the Father said of Him: "This is My beloved Son - in whom I am well pleased . . . " The Spirit descended bodily like a dove, but the focus was on the Lamb of God - who takes away the sins of the world. Not the dove, but the Lamb! Christ told His disciples of a coming Pentecost, when the Spirit would be outpoured for a single purpose: It was to be a power given to lift up the name of Christ. "But ye shall receive power, after that the Holy Ghost is come upon you: and ye shall be witnesses unto Me . . . unto the uttermost part of the earth (Acts 1:8 KJV).Jesus made it clear that when the Spirit comes He will not draw attention to Himself, but will focus on Christ's words. He will exalt Christ. When He, the Spirit of truth, is come . . . He shall not speak of Himself . . . He shall glorify Me: for He shall receive of Mine, and shall show it unto you. All things that the Father hath are Mine: therefore said I, that He shall take of Mine, and shall show it unto you." (John 16:13-15 KJV) Jesus said, "He will show you My glory, My power, My Kingdom. He will remind you of all My words." The primary work of the Holy Spirit is not fellowship, although He does bring believers together as one in Christ. It is not ecstasy. It is not simply to teach us an unlearned tongue. The Spirit has come to exalt Christ.

He Came Incognito and this SPECIAL EDITION has one sole purpose and that is to guide all mankind to the truth that Christ is Lord. It is not enough to say the Spirit has brought us close to each other - He must bring us closer to Christ. The fullness of the Spirit is the fullness of Christ. If you do not have a consuming love for Christ, you do not have a Holy Ghost baptism. The blessed Holy Spirit will be grieved, and finally withdraw the moment men try to exalt Him above the Son of God! He will not permit His power to be abused by those who want only the gift and not Christ, the Giver!

Jesus Christ is exalted at AdotcomChurch.com. It is His holiness that pierces the soul, where men and women fall before His holy throne, broken, humbled crying, "Holy, Holy. The moving of the Holy Spirit is a moving closer to Christ, deeper in Christ, with a greater submission to His Lordship!

Here it is 2013 and still Christ Is Made a Stranger in so many lives! We praise a Christ to whom we will not pray! We have become a praising people, but not a praying people. For many of God's people the prayer closet is a relic of the past. Why ask God for what He has already promised? We must get hold of the promises. We no longer want Christ as much as we want what He can do for us. We want an escape from pain and suffering. We want our troubles to vanish. We are so caught up in our escape from pain, we lose the true meaning of the Cross. We refuse crosses and losses - no Gethsemane for us. No nights of agony. We don't even know this suffering, bleeding, resurrected Christ. We want His healing power. We want His promises of prosperity. We want His protection. We want more of this earth's goods. We want His happiness. But we really don't want Him alone so He Must Come into Our Lives INCOGNITO, IN OBSCURITY.

How many of us would serve Him if He offered nothing but Himself? No healing. No success. No prosperity. No worldly blessings. No miracles, signs, or wonders. What if instead of clear sailing and problem-free living, we faced shipwreck, fears within and fighting without what if instead of painless living we suffered stoning and bloodshed? What if instead of our beautiful homes and cars, we had to wander about in deserts in sheepskins, hiding in dens and caves? What if instead of prosperity, we were destitute, afflicted, and tormented? And the only better thing provided for us was Christ? Very few of God's people pray anymore! They are too busy working for Jesus to talk to Him! Ministers especially have become so busy doing kingdom work, they have little or no time left to pray. There is time to visit, to build, to travel, time to vacation, to attend meetings, time for recreation, reading, counseling - but no time to pray! Preachers who do not pray become promoters. They become frustrated building contractors. When they lose touch with God, they lose touch with their people and their needs. Preachers who don't pray have egos that spin out of control. They want their own way. They substitute sweat for unction (anointing). Evangelists who do not pray become stars, storytellers. They lack humility, so they manipulate crowds through emotional gimmicks. The cry of many pastors is, "Oh, God, where can I find an evangelist who doesn't care about money, or who is not promoting something? One who can bring heaven down and make Christ real! Oh, God - give me a praying man to bring my congregation to its knees! The shame of this generation is that we have too many talented men and women of God and only a few who have touched God in prayer. There is even less praying in the congregation we need to be 100% for getting prayer back in our public schools.

However that's not God's real problem right now as the challenge today is getting prayer back in our homes! His problem right this minute is to get His chosen people to pray! Are you neglecting secret-closet praying?

Many of us have the formula down pat - "in the name of Jesus." All we need Him for is to countersign our petition checks before the Father. I am weary of hearing people say, "This is such a busy age - I have no time to pray. I'd like to, but I don't have time. It's not lack of time it is a lack of desire. We make time for what we really want to do.

He Came Incognito is about getting us to realize that it is He that takes the time to intercede for us before the throne of God (Heb. 7:25), and we have the nerve to say we do not have time to pray to Him! Spiritual Leaders we work feverishly for a Christ we ignore. We will go anywhere do anything, in His name. But we will not pray.

We will sing in a choir. We will visit the sick and the prisoners. But we will not pray. We will counsel the hurt and needy; we will stay up all night to comfort a friend, but we will not pray. We will fight corruption! We will crusade for morality! We will stand up against nuclear weapons! But we will not pray! Most of all, we don't pray because we really don't believe it works.

Prayer is a bloody battleground! It is where victories are won! A place to die to self! A place where a holy God exposes secret sin!

A praying man sends a shudder through hell. You become marked because our enemy knows prayer is the power that crushes his little "k" kingdom. This enemy is not afraid of power-hungry saints, but he trembles at the sound of a praying saint! Christ is made a Stranger in our midst when we want His Power more than His Purity. Those who want power, line up to my right. Those who want purity, line up to my left. Most in line will vote 10 to 1 - for POWER! In the book of Acts, Pentecost was synonymous with purity more than power. The one with the power - is the one with the purity the righteous are bold as a lion (Proverbs 28:1). The prophet Malachi prophesied of a supernatural purge coming to God's house. AdotcomChurch.com is waiting for the time our Lord is given an offering in righteousness (Malachi 3:1-3). My Bible says He is coming back for an overcoming Church, a Church without spot or wrinkle, a people whose affections are on things above a people with clean hands and pure hearts, a people who are looking for His coming.

A people with a new Jerusalem state of mind. The question is no longer, "What can my faith get me? What miracle will He perform for me?" The question now is - "How shall I stand before Him? How shall I make it at the Judgment? Who shall stand when He appears?" (Malachi 3:2) The question is no longer, "How do I feel - how do I get happiness? How do I get the desire of my heart?" The question is - "Can I withstand that moment when I stand before the Judgment Seat of Christ? how can I withstand when I've lived so carelessly, so selfishly, so neglectful of His great salvation?"

The central issue now is HAVE I NEGLECTED CHRIST IN THIS MIDNIGHT HOUR? The purge has already started in in the pulpit. He shall purify the sons of Levi (Malachi 3:3) God is going to accomplish that by "turning up the heat."

God is going to make things so hot, so fiery, so intense, God's men and women will be driven to their knees! This is the fire of the Holy Ghost! It is the fire of persecution. It is the fire of tribulation. It has already started and the fire of unbelievable hardships, ridicule, gossip, and financial problems will shake everything that can be shaken.

He is going to shake, and scrub, and burn, and purge - and purify!

No man or woman of God will escape the purging!

God is determined to get all the dross, filth, Pride and Self Righteousness out of us. The purge will spread from the pulpit to the pew! Get ready, saints! God is getting ready to expose all sin, all adultery and all foolishness. The Holy Ghost is going to reprove us of sin. How can you play games when God puts you in His crucible and turns up the fire? Your Holy Ghost baptism is going to have some fire put to it now. Malachi said - "...the day cometh, that shall burn as an oven: and all the proud, yea, and all that do wickedly, shall be stubble: and the day that cometh shall burn them up..." (Malachi 4:1).

God also promises to bring down the strongholds of the enemy. He is going to once and for all let the enemy and his world know who has the power. If God is about to do all that the prophets predicted He would - WHAT A GLORIOUS FUTURE JUST AHEAD!

AdotcomChurch.com is a purged and purified ministry we live to be a Church that God is calling back to repentance and holiness. We are a people washed, cleansed and humbled Gathering whose sole goal is to offer praises in true righteousness. We are Revolutionaries who are standing firm and calling all strongholds to come down. The sound of prayer – intercession can be heard here in Nashville, TN. We are a people of God who will discern between the holy and the unholy. We see on a daily basis God's people returning again to the Word. We are a Church Without Walls and we are a tested, tried people, once again devoted to the Person of Jesus Christ.

His Person is being lifted up to draw all men to Him. Christ no longer the stranger in our midst, but CROWNED - PRE-EMINENT!

We are AdotcomChurch.com that truly exalts the name and power of Jesus Christ, the Lord of all. In the last days, the mountain of the house of the Lord will be established as the chief of the mountains, and will be raised above the hills; and all the nations will stream to it (Isa. 2:2).

Today, in the very context of our lives and times, the first stages of this Scripture are being fulfilled. Throughout the body of Christ, leaders and intercessors are uniting in unprecedented ways. Indeed, the house of the Lord is being established. You ask just how significant is this? In the history of the Church there has never been a time when Christians from so many backgrounds came together as we do today. Our pattern has always been to divide and then criticize those with whom we once associated. Yet, today this trend is being reversed! God is establishing His house Isaiah plainly says God's house will be rebuilt "in the last days." Since the book of Acts, the church has been in the period known as "the last days." The house of the Lord is already rising above the sociological "mountains" of greed and hatred. The Lord continues to remove sin and division from our lives. When He is done, we too will see the Lord's house rise. I am amazed by the power in Isaiah's promise. He says "all the nations will stream" to the mountain of the Lord. Only in God can streams flow up a mountain. This promise speaks of resurrection life being poured out upon the nations - drawing people out of the ancestral sins and generational curses that have, for so long, weighed heavily upon us. Supernatural power is coming from the house of the Lord to reverse the "gravity" of life's situations.

Do we not often feel a downward pull, whether from work, school, world events, or cultural and moral corruption? These all weigh heavily upon us. Yet, God's word tells us that wherever the house of the Lord is built, the updraft of eternal life will inspire new beginnings for the nations streaming toward Christ. Isaiah continues, "And many peoples will come and say, 'Come, let us go up to the mountain of the Lord, to the house of the God of Jacob; that He may teach us concerning His ways, and that we may walk in His paths' " (Isa. 2:3). This, too, is happening in our day. While some may be focusing on the signs of the times, as well as the signs of renewal, still others are seeking to go deeper: to learn God's ways and to walk in His paths. For the law will go forth from Zion, and the word of the Lord from Jerusalem and He will judge between the nations, and will render decisions for many peoples" (Isa.2:3-4).The Lord is rendering "decisions for many peoples" from His house. He compels us to deal with the conflicts between us. He has decreed: Racism and Hatred cannot exist in God's house.

"And they will hammer their swords into plowshares, and their spears into pruning hooks. Nation will not lift up sword against nation, and never again will they learn war" (Isa. 2:4). Repentance is the first sign of revival; reconciliation is the second. However, the result of being upgraded to God's standards is that He accompanies us in the great harvest. Swords and spears, instruments once used against each other, are being hammered into plowshares and pruning hooks; they are becoming instruments of harvest. How Awesome is this Place called AdotcomChurch.com. An outpouring of redemptive mercy is coming from the Lord; it is streaming through His house into the world. Yes the glory of Jesus Christ be seen in His living house.

The main characteristic of AdotcomChurch.com being the Lord's house is the fact that we have a digital place where religion fades and the reality of God appears. This is where the living God has chosen to manifest Himself. "Then Jacob awoke from his sleep and said, 'Surely the Lord is in this place, and I did not know it.' And he was afraid and said, 'How awesome is this place! This is none other than the house of God, and this is the gate of heaven' "(Gen. 28:16-17). The final revelation is that the Lord's house is "the gate of heaven." There is absolutely no place on earth like the house of the Lord! It is truly an "awesome" place. So Jacob called this angelic reality, this spiritual abode where God and man could dwell together, "Bethel," the house of God (Gen. 28:19). It speaks of more than the visitation of God; this is God's habitation. The Highest Priority is to have a place of peace in God's House. Today we are praying and working for revival in our land. If we would give the restoration of the Lord's house a higher priority, if we would repair our ruined relationships and rebuild our fallen unity, we would find an ever-increasing power from God to heal our needs.

Consider the Lord's word to His disciples. He said, "You did not choose Me but I chose you, and appointed you that you would go and bear fruit, and that your fruit would remain" (John 15:16). The disciples certainly felt that they had chosen Christ. Yet the deeper truth was that God chose them before the foundation of the world. Likewise, He chose us and predestined us to come to Christ (Eph. 1:3-5). We could not even come to Christ had not the Father drawn us (John 6:44). Yet He who chose us also appointed us to bear fruit. The same power that worked in us our surrender and faith continues to work in our hearts, appointing us to bear fruit. Do you believe God has chosen you? Then believe also that He has appointed you to bear fruit.

Chap Oscar I'm just so dis-appointed with the whole church thing and my challenge to you is to remember that you just may be robbing yourself of His appointment He has for your destiny. Our appointed breakthrough remains in the heart of God. Hope deferred has made many hearts sick. It is here, even in the throes of dis-appointment that we must learn to live by faith (see Hab. 2:1-4). Disappointment cuts us off from our vision, and without a vision people perish. Are you carrying disappointment in your heart? Renounce it. Forgive those who have let you down. Have you personally or morally failed? Repent deeply and return to your Redeemer. Right now, I ask the Holy Spirit to remove the paralyzing sting of disappointment from your heart. Holy Spirit, deliver your people this day from the effect of the disappointment. Let them know that their appointment with destiny is still set.

Lord Jesus Christ is our perfect Mentor. We are all standing at a crossroads. Will this nation move toward heaven or hell? Will we see a national awakening or national destruction? I am fully convinced that when a remnant like AdotcomChurch.com truly becomes Christ-like in prayer, character and motives--we will ultimately see the glory of God fall upon our land.

That is my goal as a Co-Host on Ted Ciuba's ThinkRichRadio.com Village of Abundance Show to encourage Godly leaders. Unfortunately we simply do not have enough time to mature people spiritually on Sundays alone. We need revelation of the potential of Christ that is resident within us. Ted and I have a special relationship he has written over 30 books and is an established leader. I thank God on my knees for having Ted as the Publisher of He Came Incognito and this Special Edition. Jesus put it this way: "He who receives you receives Me, and he who receives Me receives Him who sent Me. He who receives a prophet in the name of a prophet shall receive a prophet's reward; and he who receives a righteous man in the name of a righteous man shall receive a righteous man's reward" (Matt 10:40-41). A prophet or righteous man carries in his spirit a "reward". It takes humility in a disciple to overlook the weaknesses of a leader and recognize the gift God has placed in him or her for our benefit. Our Lord only needed one Paul as long as he understood the principles of mentoring, impartation and replication.

The Book of Hebrews expands this and urges us to be careful. He admonishes, "Remember those who led you, who spoke the word of God to you; and considering the result of their conduct, imitate their faith. Jesus Christ is the same yesterday and today, yes and forever. We must choose our leaders wisely. Christ is not a doctrine or religion; there is not a different Redeemer in heaven than Christ living in us. When Christ comes into flesh, He still comes to transform the world. Listen well, for when the Spirit of Christ manifests in our world, He takes over our hearts. Christ Himself is the eternal blueprint for my life. Only in studying Him, do we grow securely upon the foundation of God. We were created to become like Christ. Some would lead us to a lesser destiny. God's plan has not become obsolete. Even as Christ has not changed, so neither has the plan of God for the Church. Our transformation will burn in God's heart "until we all attain to the unity of the faith, and of the knowledge of the Son of God, to a mature man, to the measure of the stature which belongs to the fullness of Christ" (Ephesians 4:13).

We define ourselves by what we do for God rather than what we become to Him. What pleases the Father most is not what proceeds from our hands but what rises from our hearts. He is seeking the revelation of His Son in us. I have learned that there is nothing on earth that so pleases the Father's heart as when Jesus Christ is revealed in us. It is this singular goal: the focused pursuit of Christ-likeness, and sharing He Came Incognito but He is Not Obscure Any Longer!

Thank you God for loving us, saving us, refining us, blessing us and including us in the work of your Kingdom, God We Love and Trust you!

About the Author

A man of great faith, Oscar Smith reads and studies the Word of God. He has served as a volunteer Chaplain in nursing homes, schools, and prisons. He is a trained as a Critical Incidence Stress Management Chaplain, and is a Licensed and Ordained Pastor; his mission focuses on Life Safety in the home. He lives in Nashville, Tennessee with his wife Marsha, and is the father of two sons, EJ and Henry. This is his third book.

Rev. Oscar Smith

 For more on Rev. Oscar Smith or to invite him to speak or train, visit…

www.Just1King.com

About This Book

"...With men this is impossible, but with God all things are possible" (Matthew 19:26). "For what shall it profit a man, if he shall gain the whole world, and lose his own soul?" (Mark 8:36).

One man spoke these words 2,000 years ago...and today they're as relevant as ever. *He Came Incognito* offers an exciting new look at the life of the Son of God, Jesus Christ. This book wasn't designed to disseminate information; it was written to present a Biblical revelation, one that offers an excellent boost of spiritual encouragement for those willing to heed the message. The thesis of this book is simple but profound: that He Came Incognito to bring an important message, *not* to be celebrated as a Messenger! He needed no titles, no big congregation, to validate who He was.

In a time when the very foundations of society and the economy are being shaken, the message of this book is good news. It's based on the authority of the Word of God, which declares that you can have a new beginning in every area of your life: "Therefore if any man be in Christ, he is a new creature: old things are passed away: behold, all things are become new" (2 Corinthians 5:17). All things become new in Christ. They're not patched up, not rehabilitated, but *new*!

He Came Incognito with an original plan, by which we are restored in His image and glory. This is a true change, from the inside out. He came to bring out the best in us! He Came Incognito to declare, "The thief comes to steal, kill and destroy: I am come that they might have life, and that they might have it more abundantly" (John 10:10).

Repeatedly in His Word, God confirms through examples, promises, and declarations that we *can* have a new beginning. So don't remain in your comfort zone. Don't settle for your present spiritual level. Enlarge your vision to encompass a great new beginning.

Thank you for taking the time to read this brief description.

I want to share this with you: Judges 3:31 briefly mentions a man named Shamgar, who killed 600 enemy Philistines with an ox goad. Truly, he didn't have very much going for him in this battle—just as I didn't, while I was writing this book. At times, I felt that this would be one big waste of time...and who on Earth would publish this work? But like Shamgar, I placed my pen in hand and began to write late at night until morning; and now, like him, I'm watching God work a miracle in my life today.

Our very best days are still ahead.

Remember this: many obstacles are actually opportunities for the demonstration of God's power. Accept the challenge to read this book slowly. Get out of the boat of safety, tradition, and familiarity. Put a demand on your potential. *He Came Incognito* is pioneering uncharted territories in the spiritual world.

God promises, "Behold, the former things are come to pass, and new things do I declare: before they spring forth I tell you of them" (Isaiah 42:9). We are changing from the Temporal to Eternal—from the emotional wounds of our past, to the eternal benefits of our glorious future.

As Paul points out in 2 Corinthians 4:17-18: "For our light affliction, which is but for a moment, works for us a far more exceeding and eternal weight of glory; while we look not at the things which are seen, but at the things which are not seen; for the things which are seen are temporal; but the things which are not seen are eternal."

###

Your very best days are still ahead.

Amen!

Additional Resources

Here's a poem a magnificient friend wrote that resonates with the message in this book. May it come alive for you!

Forgiveness

by Joyce E. Barrie
© 2011 Joyce E. Barrie

How do I forgive?
How do I let go?
You hurt me so bad,
And you know this is so.

How could you, I ask
I am reminded every day
The pain is so intense
It just won't go away.

You really were cruel
What you did was obscene
You left me devastated
How could you be so mean?

When truth be told
I knew that the healing key
Was to forgive you.
Not for your sake--but for me.

And so, I forgive you
But I may never forget
What you did to me
That you don't even regret.

Without this healing
Which is so dramatic
Forever my life would be
Totally traumatic.

And so, I forgive you
Though what you did was a sin
I am forgiving you
So the healing can begin.

Tune Into What The Los Angeles Times Calls "#1 Radio Show"!

Yes, this is the same lady who wrote and reads "Foregiveness", just shared with you. She's actually quite a name in the radio world...

In an episode titled "Beginning of a New Beginning," as shared on the *Joyce Barrie & Friends* **Show**, Oscar Smith, formerly "Chauffeur to the Stars," shares how he transitioned to being a practicing CISM chaplain and author of the new book, *He Came Incognito*.

Joyce E. Barrie

After hearing Oscar's story, host Joyce Barrie said the powerful words,

"He extracts wisdom and offers solid hope and comfort for times when we all are faced with challenging situations and how to successfully deal with them."

Tune in. Hear why the Joyce Barrie **& Friends** Show is the "**# 1 radio show**" as seen in the Los Angeles Times... **And** the #1 resource for extraordinary coaching and mentorship.

Joyce Barrie & Friends Show
11am EST / 8am PST weekdays
BlogTalkRadio.com/joycebarrie
Or call +1-917-388-4530
All shows in archives

Official website:

www.BlogTalkRadio.com/joycebarrie

Go From Fear To Faith!

The Source: God's Plan for Successful Spirit-Filled Living by Bobby Williams, is a must read for anyone who is facing the fears, frustrations and pressures of tough times. If your life is in a crisis situation, and you are worried and fearful about your future, then you need to read The Source.

Author Bobby Williams shares how the "Source" was revealed to him and empowered him to succeed though some of the toughest times in his life.

Bobby Williams

Read how you, too, can go from fear to faith no matter what you are facing today.

Forever changed through the transformation of prayer and study, Bobby explains the step-by-step process to a closer walk with God, the true "Source."

It can help you transform you life into a life without fear!

Find strength, peace and success through *The Source*, available at:

SpiritofaChampion.com

"He looks upon *The New Think & Grow Rich* as His workmanship!"

Ted Ciuba
Author of *The New Think And Grow Rich, 101 Quantum Success Secrets, The John Gospel Code* and more...

*"This is **more than just a revamp with modern examples** - it radically transforms the vision by adding new gender, cross-cultural and international issues to the mix, including new material to include both science and genetics, as in the Quantum reality of accelerating income and wealth. An excellent re-do of a classic financial inspirational guide."*

Rev. Oscar's Take On *The New Think And Grow Rich*

"A voice came to me, whispering, "*The New Think and Grow Rich* by Ted Ciuba is a must read!" The voice was so loud and so clear - and it rose up in me again and again.

"*The New Think And Grow Rich* really changed my life. Rereading it for the second and third time - just the revelation that's coming out of that book! And I read that book 20-30 years ago when Napoleon Hill wrote it, but Ted does a treatment in that book that really gets deep into your mindset - and all mindsets and traditions... He really has a gifting to **free you from old paradigms and old dynamics**.

Ted Ciuba is a man who looks deeper than theological degrees and correct doctrine. I profess God honors Ciuba's sustained and focused love. **He looks upon *The New Think & Grow Rich* as His workmanship!**"

Get your copy of *The New Think And Grow Rich* by Ted Ciuba at:

www.ThinkRich.com

Made in the USA
Charleston, SC
11 September 2013